Monya

The Making of a Derbyshire Village

Robert Johnston

Shirley Johnston

Published in the UK by
Horizon Editions Ltd
Trading as The Horizon Press
The Oaks, Moor Farm Road West, Ashbourne, DE6 1HD
Tel: (01335) 347349
books@thehorizonpress.co.uk

1st Edition

ISBN: 978-1-84306-524-1

British Library Cataloguing in Publication Data: a catalogue record for this book is available from the British Library.

Print: Gomer Press Limited. Llandysul, Ceredigion, Wales
Design by: Mark Titterton
Edited by: Ian Howe

Front Cover: Monyash Green and The Bull's Head
Back Cover: Fere Mere

TABLE OF CONTENTS

TABLE OF FURTHER INFORMATION BOXES

TABLE OF FIGURES

PREFACE

We have tried to design this book so that it can be used in several ways. For those wanting to read a short history of the village, each of the 35 chapters provides a short one or two page overview of the development of the village. For those wanting to dip into the book, we hope that the collection of photographs and diagrams will provide some interesting glimpses into the village and various nuggets can be picked out of the nearby text or from the chronology (time-line), the light green box at the start of the book. For those wanting a more detailed explanation of surrounding events, geology, social history, local families or population growth for example, there are 30 Further Information Boxes, light pink pages, containing much more detail.

This book began as an idea on a couple of sheets of paper some 30 years ago and slowly, very slowly, transformed into the idea for a booklet about St Leonard's Church as part of a fundraising campaign in 1985. As more and more information came to light it moved into a book about all three churches and chapels in the village, and, in more recent years, a book about the village itself.

The book started out as a labour of love, collecting information from many sources. Each source invariably provided new information and new sources to investigate. Indeed, a separate book could be written on almost every chapter. We have tried to extract, condense and simplify to create what we hope is a readable book. We are sure that as time goes by more information will be found and additions, corrections and developments made to this material.

We have done our utmost to provide acknowledgement to the work of others and to reference all information sources to enable others to follow up the material, check, challenge and hopefully develop it. All mistakes, errors, omissions, inaccuracies are ours and we would be pleased to hear of any changes and additions that should be made.

Any profits from the sale of this book will go to St Leonard's Church and the Methodist Chapel in Monyash.

We have done our best, in our spare hours, in between bringing up a family and managing our jobs, to put this book together. We hope you enjoy it.

Bob and Shirley Johnston
August 2010

ACKNOWLEDGEMENTS

This book would not have been possible without the help of many people. We are especially grateful to the following for their considerable expertise and guidance:

Mark Askey (the 1886-1888 restoration of St Leonard's Church)
Sir William Blackburne (medieval and early modern history and legal interpretations)
Simon and Judy Corble (proof reading)
Joy Davenport (prehistory, ancient and medieval history)
Chris Drage (church history and architecture)
Kathryn Johnston (maps, drawings and diagrams)
Ruth Wragg (proof reading)

Many of the late, past and present residents of Monyash and neighbouring villages have provided valuable assistance, in particular:

Jane Andrews	Bill Gee	Brenda Lomas	Peter Skinner
Mary Belfield	Maureen Gee	Colin Macdonald	John Sutton
Molly Boam	Rev John Goldsmith	Vera Naylor	Stephen Thompson
Angela Browett	Mike Harris	Chris Palfreyman	Diane Tranter
Melvyn Browett	Henry Hawley	Frank Palfreyman	The Trustees of the Ralph Rider
Teddi Carlson	Rev James Hildage	Malcolm Palfreyman	and Palfreyman Trusts
Rev Tom Comley	Doris Holmes	Alan Renfree	Hugh Tyler
Ann Comley	Jean Jackson	Eileen Slater	Jack Wake
Greg Fox (Foxline Publications)	Mary Jessop-Melland	Jim Slater	John Wood

We are greatly indebted to many people for the figures and photographs:

Michael Bentley (Figures 59, 60, 68, 69)	Ray Manley (Figure 76)
Derbyshire Times (Figures 73, 75)	Museums Sheffield (Figures 11, 12, 16, 17, 29)
Rob Faulkner (Figure 48)	The Palfreyman family (Figures 5, 6, 8, 47, 52, 53, 65, 66)
Maureen Gee (Figure 62)	Peak Advertiser (Figure 63)
Stephen Gilman (Back cover)	Peak District National Park Authority (Figures 70, 76)
Rev James Hildage (Figure 41)	Lindsey Porter (Figure 33)
Dr John R Hollick (Figure 59)	Peter Skinner (Figures 35, 37, 46, 54, 72)
Kathryn Johnston (Figures 4, 14, 15, 18, 19, 22, 24, 25, 27, 28, 31, 39)	Harry Townley (Figures 60, 68, 69)
Brenda Lomas (Figure 78)	

Our thanks also to Lindsey Porter and the highly professional team at The Horizon Press Ashbourne, for their help in bringing this project into print and for the design of the book. We are particularly grateful to Mark Titterton, the designer, for his expertise and patience.

Our sincere apologies to anyone we have missed. Please let us know and we will correct it in any future edition.

Cows in front of the old post office 2009

Fere Mere 2010

CHRONOLOGY — THE DEVELOPMENT OF THE VILLAGE

350 million years ago	The limestone under the village was laid down over millions of years.
300 million years ago	Molten lead, and other minerals, flowed into gaps in the limestone during volcanic activity in the area.
5 million years ago	Moving ice sheets deposited clay where the centre of the village is, later allowing pools of standing water.
10,000 years ago	The last Ice Age retreated and the flood waters carved out Lathkill Dale.
8000 BC	There was evidence of people living around the Monyash area.
3000 BC?	There was a henge at Arbor Low predating the current henge.
2500 BC?	The burial mound at Gib Hill was constructed.
2000 BC	The Neolithic trackway was in use and part of a long distance network.
	Arbor Low was constructed and used by Neolithic people around Monyash.
	Monyash may have been known as Manis, meaning wet lands.
Circa 1000 BC	Celtic immigrants moved into Britain bringing metal-working skills creating Early British communities.
	A simple shrine used to worship gods may have stood where St Leonard's Church is today.
	A form of the Celtic language was spoken.
	Water was venerated and wells in the village given offerings (dressed) and blessed – the beginnings of wells dressing.
800 BC	The wooded land around the village began to be cleared for arable farming.
	Tracks were developed and walls built.
Before 43 AD	The inhabitants of Monyash were part of the Brigantes tribe.
	The population of Monyash increased with improved farming methods.
	Britain traded with other parts of the world including the Roman Empire
43 AD	Roman Emperor Claudius mounted an invasion of Britain.
	Cartimandua, Queen of the Brigantes, ceded power to the Romans.
	Latin was the language of the elite.
	Mining operations began in Mandale Mine?
80 AD	The Romans created roads for their armies (including The Street near Monyash) and destroyed many religious sites.
	Lead deposits around Monyash were exploited and the village prospered.
100 AD	Christianity was widespread in Britain.
410 AD	The Romans left Britain.
410 AD onwards	Monyash was likely called Maneas, meaning many springs or waters. Old English (language) was prevalent.
600 AD	Monyash was part of the Anglo-Saxon Pecsæte 'kingdom'.
600s AD	A Pecsæte warrior was buried with his helmet near Benty Grange.
	Mercia, one of the most powerful kingdoms in Britain, annexed Pecsæte.
	The Mercian king, Penda, was converted to Christianity.
793 AD	The Viking invasions of England began.
800s AD	The Vikings occupied and ruled much of northern England (The Danelaw), and the Mercian king was ousted.
900 AD onwards	Power moved violently between Anglo-Saxon kings and the Vikings.

1066	Norman armies (with Viking origins) defeated Anglo-Saxon armies at Hastings.
	King William declared that all land was his and gave part of the Manor of Monyash to a Norman soldier, Henry de Ferrers.
1086	Monyash was referred to as Maneis in the Domesday Book.
	Monyash was a small farming community with some small-scale lead mining.
	Villagers travelled to Bakewell for church services.
	Norman French was the language of the ruling elite.
Circa 1100	The ownership of Monyash passed to William Peverel.
	A simple stone church was built in Monyash.
1113	The manor of Monyash was transferred to Lenton Abbey.
Circa 1180	The manor of Monyash was taken back by the Crown.
1191	Prince John (illegally) gave land and churches, including Monyash Church, to Bishop Hugh de Nonant, starting a 300 year legal dispute.
1199	Monyash Church was extended to include a nave and a separate chancel.
1200s	Monyash's farmers and small holders farmed small fields bounded by stone walls, surrounded by large areas of common land for sheep rearing and turf digging for fuel.
1200s?	Monyash Church was dedicated to St Leonard.
1225	The upkeep of the tracks and roads became the responsibility of landowners.
1225-1250	A two stage tower, maybe with a small spire, was added to the Church.
1236	Part of Monyash was reclaimed as Crown land, with other parts passing through various hands for many years.
1340	Monyash was granted a charter for a weekly market.
	The market cross was built on the green.
1340s	The village and the Church prospered with the growth in lead mining and income from the markets.
	Packhorse ways and drovers' roads were established through the village.
1345	St Leonard's Church acquired burial rights.
1350	Wells dressing was revived in Tissington.
Circa 1350	North and south aisles were constructed and a north transept and south transept (Lady Chapel) added to the Church.
1380	The tower was extended by a third section with a spire.
1490?	The Church's high pitch roof was lowered and Gothic arches used to support it.
1530s	King Henry VIII separated the Church from Rome to create the Church of England.
	Monyash Church and its income were seized by the Crown and the Chantry Priest pensioned off reducing education provision in the village.
Circa 1557	Monyash was sold to Sir William Cavendish.
1567	Monyash was acquired by the 6th Earl of Shrewsbury on his marriage to Bess of Hardwick, widow of Sir William Cavendish.
1577	Monyash first appeared on a map.
1579	Monyash had five pubs.
1580s	There were disputes with other villagers about the rights to dig for turf in the common lands between villages.
1616	The manor of Monyash was broken up on the death of the 7th Earl of Shrewsbury.
1650	St Leonard's Church became a parish church.
1662	Monyash had a population of around 208.
1668	John Gratton moved to Monyash, establishing a branch of the Quakers in Monyash.

1697	An Act of Parliament was passed to try to improve the condition of tracks and roads.
1700s	The Street (the old Roman road) began to fall out of use, in favour of tracks linking villages, such as Derby Lane and Horse Lane in Monyash.
Circa 1709	The guide stone on Derby Lane was erected.
1711	John Gratton died leaving his cottage to become the Quaker Chapel.
Circa 1720	Several charities were set up in Monyash to help the poor.
	Methodism came to Monyash.
1724	The London-Derby-Manchester Road became a turnpike – with tolls.
1730s	The Newcastle-under-Lyme to Hassop turnpike through Monyash (Tagg Lane and Horse Lane) had toll houses in the village.
1735	Edward Cheney became Lord of the Manor of Monyash.
1740	Magpie Mine began operating.
1740s	Polished limestone (marble) from Monyash was sold across Britain.
1742	The Royal Coat of Arms was hung in the Church.
Circa 1750	The Street (old Roman road) fell into disuse.
1752	Monyash Primary School was built from funds donated by Edward Cheney and other local landowners.
1771	The Monyash Enclosure (Inclosure) Act led to the common areas around Monyash being walled and allocated to landowners, extending the field system around the village.
	The villagers lost their access to the common land.
1776	Rev Robert Lomas met an untimely death in Lathkill Dale.
	Public rights of way were created and roads/tracks walled in.
1800s	The current spelling of Monyash prevailed.
1801	Monyash had a population of 330.
Before 1811	Monyash's fairs and markets were discontinued.
1823	The Palfreyman Trust was set up on the death of Thomasin Palfreyman.
1825	Monyash was a designated Methodist preaching location.
1831	One of the first long-distance railways was constructed from Cromford to Whaley Bridge passing close to Monyash (the Cromford & High Peak Railway – C&HPR).
1835	The original Methodist Chapel was built.
1845	Monyash markets and fairs were re-established.
1851	Monyash's population reached its peak of 473 inhabitants.
	Monyash had three pubs, including The Bull i' th' Thorn.
1846	There were over 15 different trades in the village.
1848	The Benty Grange helmet was discovered.
1849	Monyash Friendly Society was established to support the ill and poor.
1851	Only around 20 people were involved in lead mining in Monyash.
1856-1877	C&HPR ran a limited passenger service with stations at Parsley Hay and Hurdlow.
1861	Edward Cheney's great-great grandson sold the manor of Monyash at auction.
	C&HPR was taken over by London and North Western Railway (LNWR) Company.
1880	The School thrived as schooling was made compulsory for young children.
1883	The pinfold was constructed.
1886-1888	The first major restoration of the Church was undertaken with major rebuilding works and internal refurbishment.

1888	The enlarged Methodist Chapel was built.
1889	Markets and fairs had again died out.
1890	The School was enlarged and had over 100 children registered.
1899	LNWR's line was completed from Buxton to Ashbourne running services from Manchester to London.
1901	Monyash had a population of 349.
1911	The king and queen trees were planted on the village green.
1918	Rev Warden was the first car owner in Monyash.
Circa 1919	The war memorial was erected on the green.
	The Golden Lion on Church Street closed.
	The village had smithies, joiners, butchers, a chandler, a cobbler, a lace factory and its own policeman.
1920s	The telephone arrived in the village.
1930s	Electricity came to the village.
1935	Piped water came to the village.
1945	More names were added to the war memorial after the end of the Second World War.
1948	The National Health Service started and the Monyash Friendly Society disbanded.
1949	Hurdlow station closed.
1950s	Cow Mere was filled in.
1951	Monyash found itself inside the country's first national park, the Peak District National Park.
1954	Parsley Hay station closed with the end of passenger services on the LNWR.
1958	Magpie Mine ceased operations.
Circa 1960	The Reading Room closed.
1965	Monyash Bank Holiday Market was established.
1971	Parts of the track bed of the C&HPR and LNWR were turned into cycle trails.
1980	Monyash was designated as a conservation area.
1981-1988	Monyash was part of the Integrated Rural Development Scheme.
	The WI hut was replaced by the village hall.
	A children's play area was created.
	Buildings and communal spaces were renovated and developed.
	Flower rich fields and new woodland areas were planted.
	The School, with 45 children, was extended into the building next door.
1985	The White Peak Walk was started.
1986	Monyash received the Europa Nostra Award.
1993	Affordable local housing was built on Soldier's Croft.
1995	A community event called Monyash Christmas was begun.
1996	The village post office closed.
1996-2006	The second major restoration of the Church was undertaken, including repairs to the tower and walls, rewiring and internal restoration and redecoration.
2000	The millennium tree was planted on the green.
2002	Monyash's web site went live.
2006	The last shop in Monyash closed.
2010	The Royal Coat of Arms was renovated and re-hung in the Church
	Monyash had a population of around 280.

Path crossing a track near Monyash 2009

1. INTRODUCTION

Monyash is a small village in the Peak District National Park in Derbyshire, UK. The area has a reputation for beautiful scenery, pleasant walks and a peaceful environment. This tranquillity contrasts with the village's vibrant past as an important meeting place around 2000 BC, later as a watering point for drovers' animals at the intersection of several trade routes, and, for over 700 years, as a busy industrial centre supporting the local lead mining industry.

During the last five thousand years these activities, and more, have left many marks on the landscape and some of that past is still visible today. A stone circle on the outskirts of the village marks a late Neolithic/early Bronze Age meeting place. Fere Mere, a small spring-fed pond, together with several wells, provided a reliable water supply for thousands of years. Remnants of lead mines and disused limestone and marble quarries can still be found. Next to the war memorial, erected shortly after the First World War, is a market cross, the base of which dates back to the 14th century when Monyash was granted a charter to hold a weekly market (see Figure 1). In the 16th century Monyash had five pubs and three places for worship. All the buildings are still standing but only two churches (the Methodist Chapel and St Leonard's Church) and two pubs (The Bull's Head in the centre of the village and Bull i' th' Thorn on the A515) are open for business. Dominating the village green are the 'king' and 'queen' trees planted to celebrate the coronation of King George V and Queen Mary in 1911. A small plaque at the narrow end of the green is the Europa Nostra Award presented to the village in 1986 for a number of revitalisation initiatives. At the other end of the green near the Smithy Café is the 'millennium' tree, planted in 2000, with a plaque with the names of the villagers born in that year. Individually and collectively these features, both ancient and modern, provide us with glimpses into the village's rich heritage.

This book attempts to capture some of that heritage and just some of the events that have shaped the village over the last few thousand years.

Figure 1 The Smithy Café, millennium tree, The Bull's Head and market cross

2. MONYASH TODAY

Monyash is at the geographic centre of the White Peak, the limestone southern upland area of the Peak District, the UK's first national park. It is an area popular with walkers exploring the network of footpaths around the hills and dales. The village has about 280 inhabitants living in around 145 houses and lies five miles west of the market town of Bakewell. It sits in a shallow, natural hollow (see Figure 2) about 275 metres (900 feet) above sea level at the head of Lathkill Dale, surrounded by open and rolling countryside with a scattering of trees, mainly sycamore and ash. The patchwork of irregular small fields, supporting mainly sheep and some beef and dairy cattle, are bounded by dry stone walls, and criss-crossed by narrow roads, footpaths and wide green lanes.

The limestone and clay on which the village sits provides some clues as to why Monyash is here today. Carboniferous limestone consists of many horizontal layers (bedding planes) with vertical joints between them (see Figure 3). Because of these joints and gaps (fissures) limestone is permeable so this area should be devoid of water, making living and farming, particularly in years gone by, extremely difficult. However, the last Ice Age left a small deposit of clay on top of the limestone allowing ponds to form fed by springs and rainfall (see Chapter 3) thus enabling people to live here.

Figure 2 Monyash in a hollow

Monyash is likely to have been inhabited by Neolithic (New Stone Age) people (see Chapter 4) as the village had water, caves for shelter in Lathkill Dale and is located close to a Neolithic trackway and stone circle, Arbor Low (see Chapter 5). Further back in time, millions of years ago, during volcanic activity in this area, the gaps in the limestone filled with minerals, in particular lead, which provided an important source of income for the village for hundreds of years, supplementing its income from farming. The torrent of water from the last Ice Age also formed Lathkill Dale which attracts ramblers to the village today bringing in some of its current income. (For information on the geological formation of the area see Box 1: The Shaping of the White Peak.)

As a result of the standing waters and the springs that fed them, the relatively fertile fields at the top of the Dale and the lead inside the limestone, the village developed over thousands of years to become what it is today.

Figure 3 Limestone bedding planes and joints

Box 1: The Shaping of the White Peak

The White Peak is an area of carboniferous limestone that was laid down around 325 to 363 million years ago. Back then this area was a shallow sea or lagoon fringed with reefs with a wide ocean beyond. Lying around five to ten degrees south of the equator (it is now 50 degrees north) the area had a tropical climate supporting a rich abundance of marine life. Over millions of years the shells of these creatures, corals, brachiopods and crinoids, settled on the sea floor, and, after consolidation, became limestone. The bedding planes visible on exposed rock faces were caused by brief interruptions to the sedimentation process as (relatively small and quiet[2]) volcanoes erupted, centred around what is now the Matlock area, depositing volcanic lava, igneous rock, known locally as toadstone. Large quantities of minerals – heated crystalline solutions originating in the earth's crust – flowed into the gaps or fissures in the rocks.[3] The commonest minerals are galena (lead sulphide – PbS), sphalerite (zinc sulphide – ZnS), fluorite (calcium fluoride – $CaF2$), baryte (barium sulphate – $BaSO4$) and calcite (calcium carbonate – $CaCO3$). (The hot springs that are the basis of the spa waters of Buxton are heated by the remnants of the magma (molten rock) that fed the volcanoes around 300 million years ago).[4]

Towards the end of the Lower Carboniferous period, around 310 million years ago, major earth movements created the Scottish Highlands and also lifted this limestone area above sea level. The later erosion of the Highlands created large amounts of sediment which eventually washed down to the Peak District. This material consolidated into millstone grit and forms the edges and high moorland plateau of the northern Peak District. The millstone grit capping to the White Peak has since been worn away by the action of ice and water, in particular the scraping effect of ice sheets (estimated to have been around 600 metres thick[5]) during the Ice Age. The sides of the millstone grit cap are visible at Black Edge in the west and Froggatt Edge in the east. During the Ice Age (roughly two to five million years ago) two ice advances covered the Peak District. Because the ice was slow moving it did not gouge out usual glacial features such as U-shaped valleys, but it did leave some deposits of boulder clay; thus the existence of standing water in the village (see Chapter 3 on the importance of water for the village).

The third ice advance did not reach as far as the Peak District but this area would have been a frozen tundra waste in winter and flooded by melting water from the snow and ice fields in the summer. The vast volumes of water were responsible for the creation of the deep valleys and dales, like Lathkill Dale. As the ice retreated so the water table lowered and many of the dales, such as the highest end of Lathkill Dale close to the village, became dry valleys as the lower volumes of water passed through the fissures below the surface.

3. THE IMPORTANCE OF WATER

Water has played a vital role in the development of the village. Indeed the village can attribute its existence, and its name, to water (see Box 2: Monyash – The Name). Monyash has several wells and springs, essential for life in the time before piped water. Importantly, lying underneath the centre of the village is a 100 by 50 metre band of clay deposited during the Ice Age (see Figure 4). This resulted in pools of standing water, a highly unusual feature in a limestone area. Over time meres (ponds) were fashioned into the clay by the villagers to provide a constant source of water. At one time the village had five meres and at least twenty wells providing the inhabitants and their livestock, as well as passing drovers, with a plentiful supply of water right up until recent times. Only one mere now remains, Fere Mere, situated behind the Primary School; its edgings and steps, which provided easy access to the water, are clearly visible today. One well can also be seen, though securely covered, in the grounds of the Primary School. Two others, which used to have pumps, are covered by large limestone slabs, one near the telephone box and another close to the driveway behind Shepley House. The importance of water is celebrated each year when three of the wells are dressed in a tradition dating back to sometime between 1200 BC and 43 AD (see Box 3: Wells Dressing).

The meres lay in an almost straight line across the village on top of the narrow band of clay (see Figure 4). The five meres were:

1. Fere (pronounced 'fear') Mere – this is still in existence (see Figure 5 and back cover).
2. Cow Mere – which was filled-in in the 1950s and is now the School's playing field (see Figures 6 and 7).
3. Jack Mere – which was fed by Newton's Hole spring and is now the car park on Chapel Street, opposite the Methodist Chapel (see Figure 8).
4. Horse Mere – this was the smallest of the meres and was located between Cow Mere and Fere Mere and now lies below the garden of the house called Ashmere, which used to be the site of the village garage (see Chapter 31).
5. Frost Mere – this is underneath the small green opposite Old Hall Cottages. (It is named after a man named Frost who lived nearby. It was earlier known as Cobby Mere after William Hawley who lived at Mere Farm, the house next to the green. His nickname was Billy Cobby.)[6]

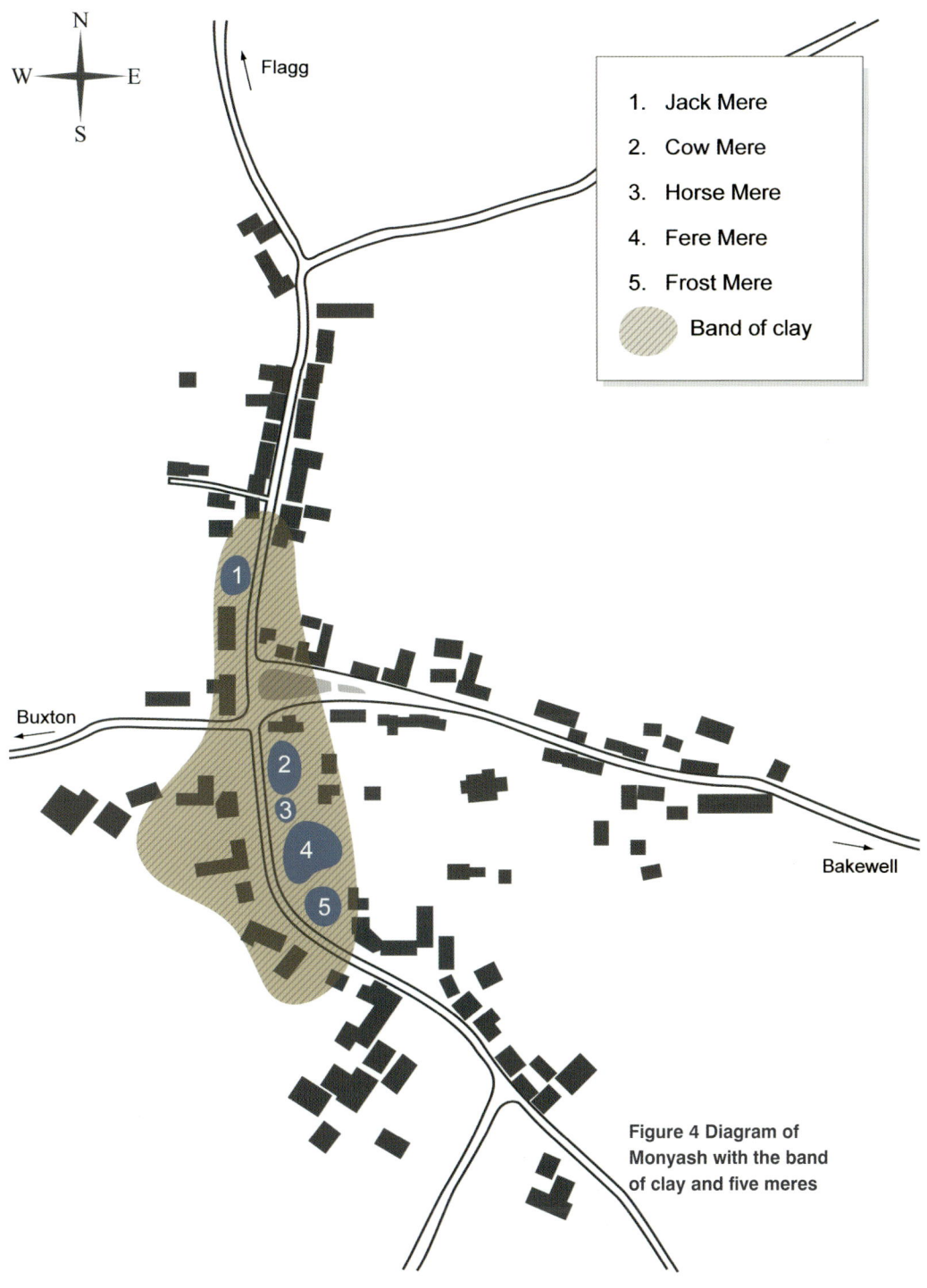

Figure 4 Diagram of Monyash with the band of clay and five meres

Figure 5 Fere Mere 1911
William Palfreyman filling his horse-drawn water cart.

Figure 6 Cow Mere circa 1910

Figure 7 Cows drinking at Cow Mere circa 1950

Figure 8 Jack Mere and the Methodist Chapel 1910

Box 2: Monyash – The Name

The signs at the entrances to the village welcome people to Monyash; however, that has not always been its name. Some sources suggest that Monyash is derived from 'many ash trees' and while this might seem reasonable given the large number of ash trees, this derivation is highly unlikely and "does not accord with the overwhelming evidence of English place-names".[7]

The name of the village was passed down by word of mouth over thousands of years, and no doubt developed over time. Even when the name was eventually written down, it was often spelt in many different ways. Indeed, different spellings can be found in the same documents. In a report on the Chantries of Derbyshire in 1545, for example, the name is spelt both as Moniasshe and as Monyashe.[8] It was not until the mid 19th century that the current spelling of Monyash started to prevail.

The very first written mention of Monyash is contained in the Domesday Book (1086) (see Box 10: Norman England and the Domesday Book and Box 11: Monyash and the Domesday Book). The village was referred to as Maneis and since then, and no doubt before, it has been spelt in many different ways including:[9]

Maneis(s) 1086, 1254-7, 1279
Manyesshes 1278
Moni-, Monyasch(e), assc(h)e, -ash(e) 1198-1208, 1215, 1285, 1545, 1605
Moni-, Mony(h)ass(e), -(h)as(e) 1200, 1236, 1243, 1251,1482
Moniax 1101-8, 1278, 1789
Monyesse 1275
Monyishe 1579
Moneyash and Money Ashe 1589, 1722, 1758, 1768, 1798

Over the last three thousand years various peoples have come into Britain – the Celts, Romans, Picts, Irish, Anglo-Saxons, Vikings and Normans – bringing with them their own cultures and languages. The result has been a merging of languages, grammatical forms and pronunciations to create the English language of today. Because of the different influences English has many quite different words with similar meanings, such as *craft* and *skill*; one derived from Old English, the other from Old Norse, or *brotherhood* from the Old English and *fraternity* from the French. It has been estimated that around 85 per cent of Old English (Anglo-Saxon) words died out as a result of the Viking and Norman invasions. However, the four or five thousand words that remained are the most fundamental words in the English language, for example, *man*, *live*, *fight*, *and*, *in*, *on*, *drink* and *eat*. Indeed, every one of the most common words in English is Anglo-Saxon (Old English) in origin.[10]

Each of those languages has contributed many place-names and influenced the forms of existing place-names. The Danish (Viking) influence was particularly strong in the north of England with over 1,400 place-names of Scandinavian origin.[11] However, the greatest influence on spelling and pronunciation happened after the Norman Conquest. There were many pronunciations in English names that were unfamiliar to the Normans. They solved this by modifying the English names to make them easier to pronounce. However, many place-names reverted back to their earlier pronunciations and spellings over time.

Many place-names have survived roughly intact over the centuries, even millennia. Monyash is one of those. Monyash, like the majority of English place-names, is at least Anglo-Saxon in origin, though given the existence of the village in earlier times, its name is likely to date back to the Iron Age (circa 800 BC to AD 43). It could even be Neolithic in origin (see Chapter 4).

In essence there are two types of English place-names, simplex and compound.[12] Simplex are local names usually referring to a single prominent feature such as a hill, valley or fort. For example Lea in Derbyshire is derived from the Old English (OE) *lēah* meaning wood, or woodland clearing.[13] Compound names are comprised of an adjective element and a topographical element. The topographical element would be an unusual or prominent feature of the landscape.

Monyash is a compound name. So if one were to take Maneis as the earliest known derivation of the name, the adjectival element *Mane* from Old English does indeed refer to *many* (from OE *manig*). Some people have assumed the topographical element, 'ash', refers to ash trees (from OE *æse*). Although the area would have been heavily wooded at one time, with a variety of trees including, and even primarily, ash, the special topographical feature for which the village was well known, and much appreciated, was its water. The *ash* part of Monyash (Maneis) was *eis* (not *ash* or *æse*) in the Domesday Book (and nearby One Ash was *Aeisc*).

The *ash* element in English place-names usually refers to water.[14] The element *eis* in Maneis is derived from the Old English *ea* (singular), *eas* (plural), meaning water(s)[15] and possibly *esce* or *æsce*, meaning spring. Thus Monyash means 'many springs' or more likely 'many waters' – referring to its life-giving pools of standing water.[16]

More speculatively one might argue it was never actually called Maneis. Maneis is somewhat clumsy and the final syllable would likely have been softened or even lost over time. Maybe it was actually called Maneas, more in line with its Old English (Anglo-Saxon) derivation, and a name that more easily rolls off the tongue. Such a mistake would not be unusual; there were no computers or spell checkers at the time of the Domesday Survey. Names were passed by word of mouth to the regional compiler, Henry de Ferrers (though his name was Henri de Ferrières), and errors in translation and transcription were not unknown. Furthermore, it is believed that *i* was pronounced *ee* and *e* more like *ay*, so Maneis, if it was Maneis at that time, would have been pronounced, rather awkwardly, as Man-ay-ee-s. Or, if it was Maneas, it would have been Man-ay-as, which is similar to today's pronunciation, which is *Munayash* rather than *Monyash* (with *Mony* pronounced like *money*).

Monyash was in existence further back in history, around 400 BC, when a form of the Celtic language was spoken in Britain and throughout most of Europe. However its many different branches split and spread and developed their own variants, so much so that Celtic (Gaelic) speakers in Scotland will most likely not understand the Celtic Welsh spoken by people just a few hundred miles away. So it is difficult to employ any of the existing Celtic languages to translate ancient place-names. However there is a view that the *eis* element might have been influenced by the Celtic for water *iska*.[17] It is suggested that *iska* became *isca* then *esca* then *esce* and *æsce* (similar to the Celtic Irish *esc* and *easc* for water).[18]

Even further back in time in the Neolithic period, and perhaps before, the area around Monyash was already inhabited. The original language spoken by Neolithic people is referred to as Proto-Indo-European. As these people fanned out across Europe they split into many different areas giving rise to several variations of Proto-Indo-European (PIE), which became the bases for future languages, including Celtic, German, Hindi, Greek, Latin, Sanskrit and Bengali.

The word *mere*, for example, that we use to describe the pond in Monyash is believed to be derived from the PIE word *mori*, meaning water. Importantly, *mani* in PIE is thought to have meant 'wetland', which may well have described the area in the centre of Monyash long before the meres were fashioned from the 'swamps' that sat on top of the bed of clay across the village. Maybe Monyash, in Neolithic times, was known as Manis, meaning wetlands.[19]

Box 3: Wells Dressing

Water is the reason for the existence of the village and its standing water (meres), springs and wells are a vital part of its heritage which are celebrated each year by Wells Dressing. The dressing and blessing of wells is a custom confined primarily to the Peak District and is an annual tradition in Monyash as it is in many Derbyshire villages. Wells *blessings* originally started as a thanksgiving for the gift of water. As a pagan ceremony, dating back two and a half thousand years (see Box 5: The Early Britons), it is believed to have originated from Mediterranean countries where water was valued not only for drinking, but also for cleansing and healing.

The *dressing* of wells with garlands of flowers or more elaborate structures may also date back to the Early British times or the practice might have been introduced into Britain during the Roman occupation. At some point the practice died out and it is believed to have been re-introduced into the Peak District at Tissington either in 1350, when Tissington was thought to have escaped the Black Death because of the exceptional purity of its water, or in 1615 when the village's wells never ran dry in a year of drought.

Wells Dressings are intricate pictures depicting inspiring scenes created from local natural materials such as flower petals, mosses, leaves, twigs and small stones, which are pressed into a clay base within a wooden frame. A week before the dressings go up the wooden frames, or boards, ranging from half a metre to two metres high, are soaked in water overnight. They used to be soaked in the mere, but now buckets of water are poured over them. The clay is then 'puddled' (mixed with water and worked into a soft consistency) and pressed, about half an inch thick, into the boards which have nails protruding to ensure the clay keys to the boards. The clay used to be sourced locally but is now supplied by a factory in the Potteries. A full size drawing of the agreed design is then laid over the clay and the design is then 'pricked out' using knitting needles to prick through the drawing to produce a clear outline of the design on the clay. Over the next few days and nights a number of volunteers, children and adults, painstakingly press each petal or piece of moss onto the damp clay to create the finished dressing (see Figures 9 and 10).

Three dressings are erected close to wells in Monyash on the Saturday at the start of the May bank holiday week. The Church now plays a part in this ancient, pagan ceremony as the vicar leads a band of villagers in a procession blessing the wells. The dressings remain in place for seven days with collecting boxes for donations to the year's chosen good causes.

Pictures of the Monyash dressings can be found on www.monyash.info/wells.php

Figure 9 A well dressing in construction
Shirley Cantrell, Sheena Moffat and Ruth Wragg creating the border for the 2010 well dressing

Figure 10 The 2008 well dressing

4. MONYASH – THE FIRST INHABITANTS

Following the end of the last Ice Age, around 10,000 years ago, people migrated to Britain while it was still joined to the rest of Europe. As the weather warmed up, becoming much warmer and drier than it is today, around 3750-1750 BC (the Neolithic Age), people colonised some of the uplands of the Peak District. However, there is evidence of people living in the area much earlier; indeed the Peak District is believed to be one of the oldest settled upland areas in the UK.[20] A double-edged stone axe-head dating back to 8000 BC was found in 1830 in a rock fissure in Calling Low Dale, just a mile from the village.[21] One Ash cave on the outskirts of the village is believed to have been inhabited even earlier.[22]

There is evidence of a number of Neolithic settlement sites around the Peak District. These tend to be on the higher ground, as evidence of lower sites is more likely to have been destroyed due to later settlements and more intensive cultivation. The largest nearby Neolithic sites are thought to have been around the Brassington, Middleton and Wirksworth area. There was a small one near Five Wells between Taddington and Chelmorton and larger ones at Lismore Fields in Buxton and Gardom's Edge above Baslow. The site at Monyash is much smaller and is spread out around the head of Lathkill Dale. Neolithic finds, flint arrowheads, tools and bowls, have been made around Monyash at Stoney Low (towards Magpie Mine), at Arbor Low, Bole Hill (near Bole Hill Farm), Haddon Grove and Calling Low Dale (see Figure 11).[23] Several flints have also been found in the fields around Monyash by resident Thurston Goodwin, who died in 1979. Some of the artefacts are housed in Weston Park Museum, Sheffield.

It is likely that Monyash was occupied by some of the Neolithic labour that built Arbor Low (see next chapter), as well as farmers who cultivated the relatively deep and fertile soils at the head of Lathkill Dale, as it provided not only a sheltered position, but also a supply of fresh spring water and standing water. It has been suggested that "on the limestone plateau, the most sheltered areas of land with the best soils are those on either side of the main river gorges and at the gorge heads [like Monyash]. These have probably been extensively used for agriculture and settlement since pre-history".[24]

Neolithic people were farmers who used a range of stone and flint tools to cultivate the fields around their settlements. One polished stone axe (see Figure 12), made from local stone, a coarse basaltic rock, was found at nearby Arbor Low (see next chapter).[25] They reared livestock, but would have also hunted wild boar and deer in the well-wooded area on the limestone plateau around Monyash. They would also have taken advantage of the wild animals visiting the area for water. Later immigrants, around 2800 – 1900 BC, the 'Beaker' people, brought with them new styles of pottery, improved flint tools, new weapons and better construction techniques. (The 'Beakers' is a name given to traders in bronze and other goods from mainland Europe who settled within local Neolithic communities.)

Figure 11 Two pots and a bone pin from Gib Hill barrow at Arbor Low

Figure 12 Neolithic polished stone axe found at Arbor Low

5. ARBOR LOW AND THE NEOLITHIC TRACKWAY

Figure 13 Arbor Low

Neolithic people built long barrows, from stones and soil, as communal burial chambers for their dead. They also constructed stone and timber circles like Stonehenge. Indeed Monyash has its own stone henge, Arbor Low, one of the best examples of a prehistoric henge in Britain (see Figure 13). It is situated at the edge of the parish of Monyash, two miles south of the village, almost at the summit of the long ridge separating the rivers Derwent and Dove. Although the precise purpose of henges is uncertain, it is likely that they were used for trading (exchange) activities, ritual ceremonies and the worship of pagan gods. Arbor Low would have served the needs of the Neolithic population living on the plateau between Monyash and Aldwark.[26] Other henges, probably serving other communities, included Staden near Buxton and the Bull Ring at Dove Holes, which was about the same size as Arbor Low.[27] (For more information see Box 4: Arbor Low.)

It is sometimes assumed that Neolithic people's main routes usually followed upland ridges, referred to as ridge-ways. However it is believed that most Neolithic tracks followed valleys,[28] making use of rivers which then gave them direct access to larger rivers, then estuaries and then to the sea and on to other parts of the country and, indeed, other countries.[29] Evidence has been found in the form of "logboats dating from every period from the Mesolithic (8500 to 4000 BC) onwards".[30]

Monyash lies just off a Neolithic upland path or trackway on high ground passing by Arbor Low.[31] This track linked Arbor Low and many other henges (stone circles) and lows in the area (low or law, from the Old English *hlāw* or *hlæw*, meaning rounded hill, sometimes the location of tumuli, Bronze Age burial mounds).[32] Five miles south on the track from Arbor Low is Minninglow (a large prehistoric burial site with four or five separate burial chambers) and further south are several prehistoric settlements near Wirksworth. Going seven miles north from Arbor Low, there was a henge at Staden, just south of Buxton. This track then passes another henge, the Bull Ring near Dove Holes. The 12 miles of almost straight track, from Staden in the north to Minninglow in the south, has around 20 tumuli on or close to its path, with over 100 tumuli marked on the Ordnance Survey Outdoor Leisure 24 map two miles either side of the track. It is likely that there would have been a path from Arbor Low, through Monyash and down Lathkill Dale, then joining up with the River Wye.

It is important to realise that these tracks were not just for local use, but formed part of a network of long-distance routes along which goods were moved between communities during the 3rd millennium BC.[33] The Bull Ring at Dove Holes was thought to be at the intersection of three routes, one from Wirksworth, via Minninglow and Arbor Low in the south, a north-east route going up Rushup Edge to Mam Tor then Win Hill and towards the Sheffield area, and another going west, probably towards the coast (see Figure 14). This trackway linked up with the River Mersey via Buxton (the west coast route) and also the River Humber, via the Rivers Wye, Derwent and Trent on the other side of the country (the east coast route). The Humber estuary is believed to have been an ancient port and three plank-built boats for river travel were found at North Ferriby, Humberside, one of which has been dated to around 1430 BC.[34] (An ocean-going boat dating to around 1100 BC has also been found near Dover.[35])

Over these routes were brought polished stone axes from the Langdale quarries in the Lake District which were used to clear the forests around Monyash. Later Bronze Age goods from Ireland came via the west coast route. Copper from nearby copper mines may well have been taken out of the Peak District over these routes, and lead somewhat later in Roman times.

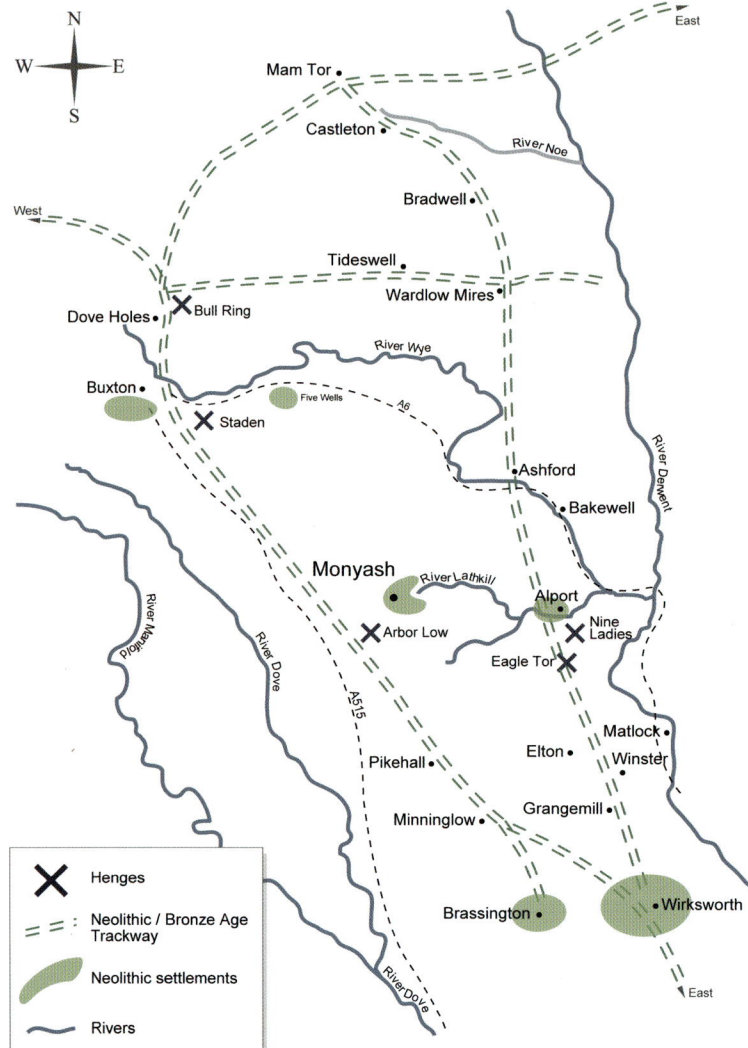

Figure 14 Neolithic and Bronze Age trackways

Box 4: Arbor Low

Arbor Low is one of the country's largest later Neolithic henges (a stone circle surrounded by a ditch) constructed around 2000 BC.[36] Nearby is Gib Hill, an associated barrow of uncertain date.

Arbor Low appears to be part of a larger complex. Gib Hill, 300 metres south-west of Arbor Low, is a burial mound and may have been the original focus of ceremonial activity. It was excavated in 1845 and found to contain cremated remains and various grave goods, including baked earth pots and a bone pin (see Figure 11), which are now in Weston Park Museum, Sheffield. Excavations near Gib Hill suggest that there may have been an even older henge on this site around 180 metres in diameter surrounded by a ditch and outer bank. This henge was located much closer to the Neolithic trackway and may have been replaced by Arbor Low to cope with an increase in the population using it.[37]

Henges appear to have been used for lavish festivals and special artefacts have been found buried within and around them, as at Arbor Low. Rituals associated with birth, puberty, marriage and death were probably carried out there, along with those connected with summer and winter solstices. It is thought that the winter solstice may have been one of the most important celebrations of the year, when the dark hours finally stopped increasing and the population could celebrate the start of a new growing season, more than likely with sacrifices to the gods. Given their proximity to major prehistoric trackways henges may also have been used as centres for trading activities.[38]

Like Stonehenge, Arbor Low began as a simple bank and ditch henge, possibly with a ring of wooden posts. At some time later large limestone blocks, from a local quarry, were brought to the site. The henge consists of about 50 large limestone blocks. However, some of the stones are broken and there may have originally been only 41 to 43 stones. The stones range from 1.6 to 2.1 metres tall, with the monoliths (large entrance stones) between 2.6 and 2.9 metres. In the centre of the circle are seven smaller blocks (see Figure 13). It is believed the stones were never standing stones like those at Stonehenge, since no holes have been found in which the vertical stones could have stood.[39] This may have been intentional, or perhaps the project was never completed. Other sources suggest that the stones were standing and have fallen or been pulled down.[40] It has been estimated that it would have required several million man-hours to construct this henge.[41]

The stones are set on an inner platform 52 by 40 metres in size, which is surrounded by an oval earthen bank, approximately 90 by 85 metres at the outside edges and two metres high, with a surrounding ditch being about two metres deep and between seven to ten metres wide. At one time the bank may have been a couple of metres high, preventing any rituals from being seen from outside.[42] There are two causeway entrances breaching both the bank and ditch; the north-west one is nine metres wide and the south-south-east one (not quite opposite) is six metres wide.[43] There is also evidence of a ceremonial approach to the henge from the nearby Neolithic trackway.

6. BRONZE AGE AND IRON AGE COMMUNITIES

During the Bronze Age (around 2500 to 800 BC) the climate deteriorated becoming much wetter forcing the population away from the uplands into the more sheltered valleys. Exhausted soils on the higher ground, farmed over the previous centuries, may also have been a factor in encouraging the population to move down into the more fertile lower ground. However, some of the higher level farms, like those around Monyash, continue to be worked to this day. A second, lower level, prehistoric track may already have been in use at this time (see Figure 14), later called the Portway, linking Wirksworth with Mam Tor, via Ashford and Wardlow, crossing the River Lathkill at Alport. This route runs close to many Bronze Age stone circles much smaller than the Neolithic ones, such as at Arbor Low, but impressive nonetheless. Examples are found at Nine Ladies on Stanton Moor and several smaller ones around Harthill Moor.

During the Late Bronze Age and the Iron Age (circa 800 BC to AD 43) the Early Britons (see Box 5: The Early Britons) created more settlements by clearing larger areas of woodland. The wood was used to construct timber roundhouses and other shelters and to provide fuel for cooking. The land was demarcated by tracks, ditches and walls, and a system of mixed arable farming was used and a range of livestock reared (pastoral farming), with sheep and cattle kept on the upland areas, such as Monyash.

The Romans identified around 27 'tribes' living in Britain at the time of the Roman Conquest, AD 43,[44] though the 'tribes' would be better described as loose confederations. The inhabitants of Monyash lived on the edge of three tribal areas; the Brigantes, the Corieltauvi (or Coritani), and the Cornovii. The Brigantes (the name means 'upland people' or 'hill dwellers') were a federation of the hill-dwelling communities of the Pennines. They were one of the biggest tribes in Britain at the time of the Roman Conquest and their area was thought to stretch from southern Scotland to the southern Pennines. The Corieltauvi (or Coritani) were based around what is now the East Midlands, and the Cornovii lived around the modern counties of Staffordshire, Shropshire and Cheshire.[45] Monyash may have belonged to all of them at various times as they tried to expand their territories. Indeed the number of hillforts in the area that were constructed around 1000 BC suggests that the Peak District was under frequent pressure from invading tribes. Nearby hillforts include Mam Tor near Castleton (possibly a southern boundary for the Brigantes), Castle Naze near Chapel-en-le-Frith, Markland Grips near Cresswell, Fin Cop overlooking Monsal Dale, Burr Tor (now the home of the Derbyshire and Lancashire Gliding Club near Hucklow), Combes Moss near Dove Holes, Castle Ring at Harthill, Gardom's Edge near Baslow, Crane's Fort near Conksbury and Ball Cross at Bakewell.[46] While some of these appear to be defensive sites, others, such as the one at Bakewell, were little more than enclosed farmsteads.[47]

Monyash might have been an important place at this time. Its farming community was sheltered by hills with animals to hunt and no shortage of supplies of wood. Importantly it had fresh and standing water and also veins of valuable lead in the limestone around the village. Despite the poor weather and the raiders, it is likely that the population of Monyash and the White Peak area grew during the Iron Age. This growth was made possible by the introduction of new and improved crops and the introduction of the iron-tipped 'plough' which eased cultivation. Land was cleared to create larger farms and dry stone walls built around the fields. The area around the village may have well looked not too dissimilar from the way it does today, with some of the dry stone walls around the village dating back to this time. One might even speculate that Monyash had its own 'fort'. The field bounded on two sides by the sharp bend in the road towards Buxton, Tagg Lane, bears some of the hallmarks of an Iron Age fort.

Box 5: The Early Britons

The Early Britons (sometimes referred to as Celts) were of Indo-European descent and spoke some form of the Celtic language, the ancestor of the main European languages.[48] From around 1000 BC several waves of Celtic immigrants moved to Britain from Central Europe.[49] By 300 BC they inhabited an area stretching from Spain in the west, through northern Europe to Asia Minor.

Before the Iron Age, implements were made from bronze, an alloy of copper and tin. Neither was easy to come by, though there was a copper mine at Ecton which has been worked for perhaps 3,000 years. Other more recently worked copper mines were at Royledge, Mixon, Hill House and Cauldon (Caldon Low).[50] The Iron Age (circa 800 BC to AD 43) saw the gradual introduction of iron tools and equipment, although the general adoption of iron artefacts did not become widespread in Britain until after approximately 400 BC. The Early Britons were skilled craftsmen. The smiths, who had a high status in tribal society, produced tools for other crafts and for farming, such as the iron-tipped ard (a simple wooden scratch-plough), bronze household equipment and iron swords, which were sharper and more efficient than bronze ones.

The Early Britons had their own calendar and worshipped many gods in the form of the forces of nature, which is not surprising given their lives revolved around cultivation and animal rearing. The sky, sun and moon and meteorological phenomena such as thunder were associated with spirits and topographical features such as hills, rivers and springs were deified as gods and endowed with divine characteristics.[51] Their ceremonies took place in forest groves – clearings endowed with spiritual properties, probably around simple shrines.[52] They would have regarded the springs and wells as sacred sites and would have given them offerings on a regular basis.[53] This pagan ritual continues to this day in the form of Wells Dressing (see Box 3: Wells Dressing), though it is now led by a Church of England priest.

Tribal leaders were renowned for their horsemanship and their warriors were armed with long slashing swords and spears which they used from horseback. The rank and file had no body armour or helmets and so were no match in AD 43 for the determined and highly disciplined invading Roman infantry.[54]

When the Romans invaded Britain they set about destroying indigenous religious centres along with their priests (sometimes referred to as druids) in order to ensure they removed an order that may have undermined their conquest.[55] Later, the early Christian Church took a different view. In AD 601 Pope Gregory told Augustine (see Chapter 9) that while pagan idols were to be destroyed, "their temples should be preserved and through fitting ceremonies converted into Christian churches".[56] Changing religious practice was clearly a slow process. A decree of AD 960 attempted to forbid the worship of fountains, yet in AD 1102 St Anselm was still condemning this practice.[57] While some rituals were eventually stamped out, many others, such as wells dressing have continued – assuming Christian significance.

The Early Britons (apart from those in the far south-west, the north of England and in Scotland) were then subject to a thousand years of invasions (see next chapter). As a result the British were pushed to the extremes of the country – Ireland, Scotland, The Isle of Man, Wales and Cornwall – where derivations of the Celtic language survived as Irish, Scots Gaelic, Manx, Welsh and Cornish. It is possible that 'Celtic' blood survived even after those successive invasions in other remote areas, so some of the families in Monyash may be of 'Celtic' descent.[58]

7. A THOUSAND YEARS OF INVASIONS

For one thousand years the British Isles were subject to waves of brutal invasions. The first invaders were the Romans around AD 50 followed by Angles, Saxons, Jutes, Vikings and Normans.

The Romans changed suddenly from trading partner to ruler (see Box 6: The Roman Invasion). They knew the names of many British tribes and set about conquering them one at a time knowing they were fiercely independent and rarely co-operated, even in the face of a common enemy. The Romans met with some considerable resistance, in particular from the Iceni (in East Anglia) and their ruler, Boudica (or Boudicca), who eventually met a violent end. However, Cartimandua, Queen of the Brigantes (and Monyash), was pro-Roman and was well rewarded for it. Her ex-husband was less willing and raised an army and made several invasions of her Roman-ruled kingdom. His last one, in AD 69, was successful and no more was heard of Cartimandua. The Brigantes then tried to repel the invading Roman army but were defeated.

As the Romans advanced northwards through England towards York they built a fort called Derventio at Little Chester/Chester Green by a crossing over the Derwent (now part of the northern suburbs of Derby).[59] From Little Chester they pushed north to quell the Brigantes, developing existing trackways or building roads as they went. Roman roads run from Little Chester to Chesterfield, to the Mersey via Rocester and Newcastle under Lyme and to Manchester via Buxton. The Roman road linking Little Chester to Buxton was called The Street, which runs past Monyash (see next chapter). (The Romans called Buxton Aquae Arnemetiae, meaning spa of the goddess of the grove, where they constructed baths using the warm spring water.) By AD 80 the Romans occupied this area and had a secure network of support and supply routes in place covering the Midlands and the north of England.[60]

When the Peak District came under Roman control with the establishment of a number of forts linked by their military roads, it is likely that some of the local population prospered. Indeed a small hoard of Roman coins was discovered close to the village.[61] The Romans were interested in the Peak District mainly because of the rich veins of lead (see Box 6: The Roman Invasion). It is possible that some inhabitants of Monyash worked in the larger lead mines, maybe Mandale Mine; others may have supplemented their income from farming with small-scale lead digging around the village.

After the Romans armies left Britain in AD 410 to deal with problems at home, the Roman way of life continued for some time. However, central rule slowly faded, paving the way for invasions of Angles, Saxons and Vikings. Raids by the Germanic Angles and Saxons began in earnest around the middle of the 5th century. The Angles formed the kingdoms of Kent, Northumbria, East Anglia and Mercia, starting their royal dynasties. These Anglo-Saxon kingdoms (as they were referred to by the Normans) then spread throughout England (see Box 9: Anglo-Saxon England).

By the 7th century Monyash was part of Pecsæte, covering the central and northern part of the Peak District (see Figure 15). One rare find from this Early Medieval period was from a barrow at Benty Grange on the outskirts of Monyash. The 'Benty Grange' helmet probably belonged to an important member of the ruling Pecsæte and was found along with some chainmail, a leather cup with silver fittings and some silver plate.[62] (See Box 7: The Benty Grange Helmet.)

By the 8th century Pecsæte had become part of the Kingdom of Mercia (see Figure 15). Mercia was ruled by a succession of kings, one of the most famous being Offa (thought not to be his real name but a family or pet name) who ruled from AD 757 to 796. The last King of Mercia was Burgred who reigned from AD 852 until 874 when parts of Mercia were invaded and occupied by the Danes/Vikings.

The Vikings arrived towards the end of the 8th century and for some time had complete control over York and the kingdom of East Anglia, and the areas around the fortified towns of Derby, Leicester, Lincoln, Nottingham and Stamford. This was The Danelaw - the land ruled by the Danish invaders. Their impact is thought to have been limited in the Peak District, though their legacy still remains in a few place-names, for example Lathkill is Scandinavian (Old Norse) from *hlatha* (a barn) and *gyll* (a narrow valley).[63]

For the ensuing years, power alternated violently between Danes and the various Anglo-Saxon kings. The situation was made worse by the continuing rivalry between the Anglo-Saxon kings themselves. In 825 Egbert, King of Wessex, defeated the King of Mercia and then, in 828, he also took control of Northumbria to become Bretwalda (overlord of some or all of the Anglo-Saxon kings).[64] With a more united country Egbert's grandson, Alfred the Great, was able to wage a stronger war against the Danes, but it was not until the end of the 10th century that Athelstan, Alfred's grandson, succeeded in driving out the Danish invaders (see Box 9: Anglo-Saxon England).

The last 'ruler' of Mercia (and Monyash) was an Earl, Eadwine. He ruled Mercia from AD 1062 to 1066 when he was forced to submit to William the Conqueror.[65]

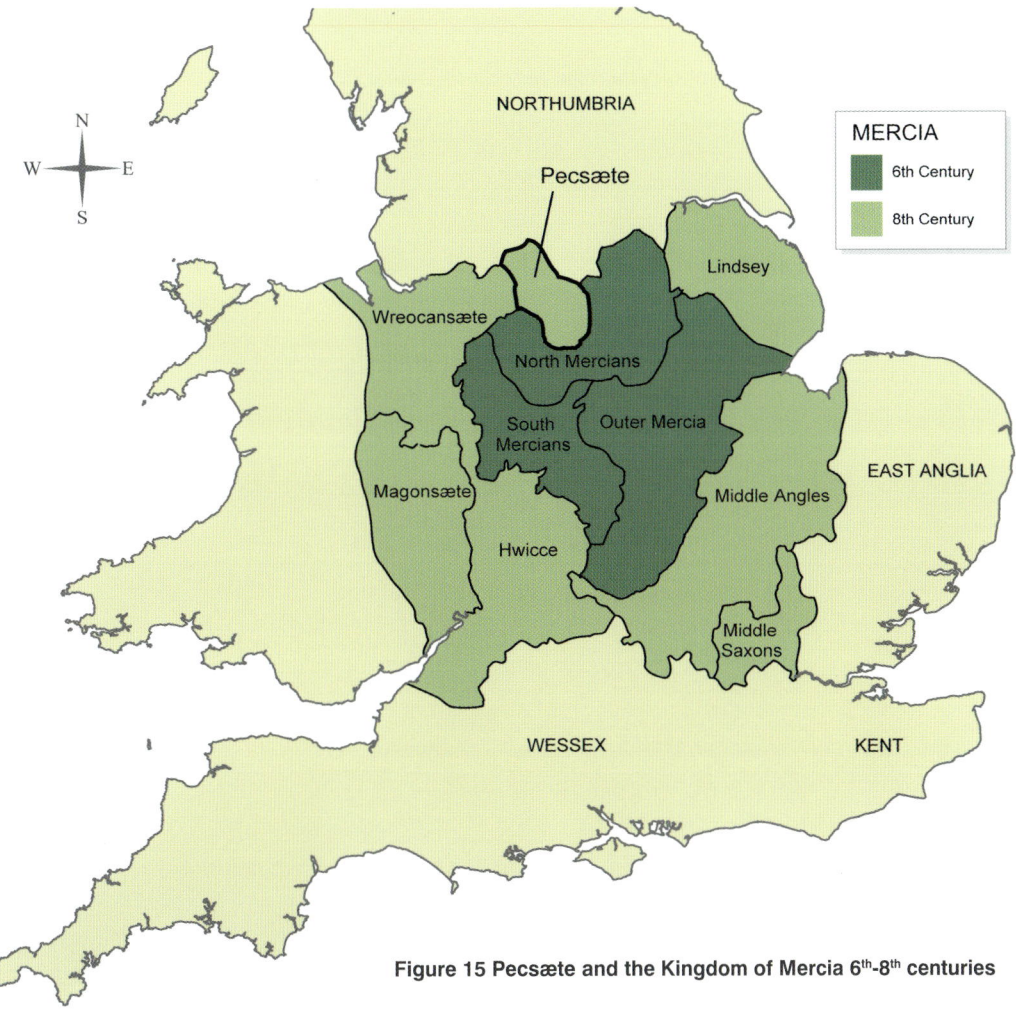

Figure 15 Pecsæte and the Kingdom of Mercia 6th-8th centuries

Box 6: The Roman Invasion

Prior to the Roman invasion, Britain already traded with the continent, particularly through Hengistbury Head near to what is now Bournemouth, importing wine, tools and pottery.[66] Emperor Caesar, around 55 BC, established trading links with some of the southern and eastern tribes of Britain. The Romans used the port of Colchester and later London, which had become a major commercial centre by AD 60. Trade from Rome was likely to have been in luxury goods such as wine which was traded for grain, cattle, gold, silver, iron, hides, slaves and hunting dogs.[67]

The Roman invasion and conquest of Britain was more a war of prestige rather than one of economics.[68] Little could be gained as trade was already well established, but Emperor Claudius saw it as a chance simply to extend his empire and influence. Following two unsuccessful incursions (or reconnaissance trips) by Caesar in 55 and 54 BC, Claudius mounted a full-scale invasion in AD 43, despite some of the British kings suggesting that he would have greater financial rewards from continuing trading with Britain than by conquering it.[69]

The Romans failed to occupy the whole of Great Britain. England was under Roman rule; Ireland was never occupied and the Caledonians and other tribes of Scotland (popularly called the Picts) managed to prevent full-scale occupation. (It was not until 1603 that Britain became a united country when King James VI of Scotland, son of Mary Queen of Scots, became James I, the first King of Great Britain, on the death of the childless Elizabeth I, Queen of England and Ireland, Mary's cousin).

The Romans called their new province Britannia and at first used puppet rulers, British tribal leaders, such as Cartimandua of the Brigantes. But quite soon Rome took over the running of the country. Latin was the language of the government, the Church and probably the army, but most people would have spoken a form of Celtic language.

The Romans were particularly interested in the Peak District because of its lead. Lead "was extensively used in the building trade for water pipes, bath linings, roofing and for hot water tanks. Plumb-bobs (from the Latin plumbum for lead) and weights were made of lead, as were some coffins and containers for cremated remains". Later pewter, an alloy of tin and lead, became increasingly important.[70] Lead was also mined for its small silver content which is produced as a by-product of lead refining. Lead was cast into inscribed moulds before leaving the mines. These lead pigs weighed 80 to 90 kilogrammes.[71] The mine workings were under Roman control though they may have been managed by Romano-British inhabitants.

The Roman Empire reached its peak during the 2nd century AD and the following 200 years saw the slow decline of its control over its territories, as well as its own crumbling institutions. The Roman armies were pulled out of Britain in AD 410 to deal with unrest at home. The Roman way of life continued for many years in Britain with Roman style developments taking place at Cirencester and Winchester for example. However, without the central authority and control of Rome, a power vacuum emerged that was to be fought over for the next 600 years.

Box 7: The Benty Grange Helmet

The Benty Grange helmet was discovered by Thomas Bateman (see Figure 16). Thomas' grandfather, also Thomas, had made his fortune in Manchester as a cotton merchant. He purchased the estate of Middleton by Youlgreave and built Middleton Hall. His son, William Bateman (1787-1835), a noted archaeologist, excavated many Derbyshire barrows. William's son, Thomas (1821-1861), carried on his father's work excavating over 200 barrows in his short lifetime. Some of his findings are now housed in Weston Park Museum, Sheffield.[72] In 1848 he discovered the Anglo-Saxon helmet in a grave at Benty Grange on the outskirts of Monyash.

This is a remarkable example of a warrior's helmet, with iron bands coming down from the top of the helmet held together by a circular brow band. The helmet would have been covered by slices of horn, secured by silver pins. It was topped by small boar made from bronze and originally covered in silver gilt with garnet (gemstone) eyes. The boar was a pagan symbol sacred to the goddess Freo (or Frigg, Freya or Frijjō – the Goddess of Spring, fertility and love; she is also associated with war and wealth). Nearby Friden is also named after Freo, the place-name meaning valley of the goddess Freo – presumably there was a place for pagan worship here. The boar on the helmet also represents

Figure 16 The remains of the original Benty Grange helmet

Photography Copyright Museums Sheffield. Reproduced with the kind permission of Museums Sheffield.

Figure 17 A replica of the original Benty Grange helmet

prosperity, vitality, strength and ferocity. However, also on the helmet is a small silver filigree (delicate wire-work) cross on the nasal protector, recognising the 'new' Christian religion. This suggests that the pagan warrior chief who wore the helmet may have been an early convert to Christianity but had not abandoned his pagan beliefs – he had also been buried with grave goods, which would be unusual for a Christian burial.[73]

In his grave was also found a small portion of his hair, traces of a silk garment and a woollen cloak and some chain mail, together with the remains of a leather cup, silver ornaments and two silver crosses. No weapons were found but they may have been removed by previous 'visitors' to the grave.[74]

Figure 17 shows a picture of the helmet and how it might have looked. The replica was made by artisan, Martin Murphy, using original methods and materials where possible. Slices of horn were heated, steamed and moulded to form the inside part of the helmet, producing a comfortable cap, to which the iron bands were attached with small, silver axe head pins. The silver-gilded boar had a slit down its back, presumably filled with a plume of boar's hair, though on this replica pig's hair is used instead.

8. THE ROMAN ROAD

There was a Roman road on the outskirts of Monyash. The Roman roads linked major Roman sites and were used for swiftly moving armies and supplies, so they were laid out as straight as possible. They usually kept to high ground and indeed the one passing by Monyash is along a ridge and some of it was built along the Neolithic trackway (see earlier). The Roman roads were well constructed with ditches either side. Large stones would form the base, topped with smaller stones and gravel to produce a cambered, well-draining and heavy duty surface (see Figure 18). The Roman road close to Monyash, next to Arbor Low, was called The Street. This was not a major Roman highway; such highways were paved and up to 12 metres wide. The Street was a secondary route; a mere six metres wide.[75]

It is tempting to think that this Roman road followed the current line of the A515, south of Monyash, where it runs straight for almost two miles. In fact the only part of the current A515 which follows the Roman (and indeed Neolithic) road is the short stretch between Street Farm (near Pomeroy Cottages and The Duke of York pub) and The Bull i' th' Thorn. At this point, going south, it would have followed the line of The Bull i' th' Thorn (which is at a slight angle to the A515) then taken a straight line across the field, past Endmoor Farm at the top of Tagg Lane, past Middle Street Farm and Benty Grange, then close to Gib Hill by Arbor Low (close to the location of the older henge) then direct to Pikehall (which was probably a Roman posting house where horses would have been changed), past Minninglow, then Carsington, Kirk Ireton and Derby – see Figure 19. (The road is clearly marked on the Ordnance Survey Outdoor Leisure 24 – Peak District White Peak Area.)

The Roman road network continued to be used in Anglo-Saxon times for moving armies and goods. It was also used to define areas of land. In AD 884 Alfred the Great, for example, used it to define the areas to be covered by Danelaw, so too did the later Saxon shire reeves (sheriffs) and bishops when defining the boundaries of the shires and hundreds (hundreds are said to be the size of land sufficient to sustain one hundred families). Some of these boundaries would later become parish boundaries;[76] indeed Monyash's western boundary lies along the line of the old Roman road. (In Monyash, because the area had been under Viking rule, the land was divided into the Danish equivalent of hundreds, wapentakes, which were later renamed hundreds.) In AD 963 Edgar, King of England (and great grandson of Alfred the Great), gave some land in the Peak District, close to Friden just a few miles south of the village, to a layman, Æthelferth. Edgar used the Roman road to set out one of the boundaries of the land, referring to The Street as King Street.[77]

While The Street, or King Street, continued to be the main road from Derby to Manchester until the 1700s (see Chapter 31) a number of other tracks became well established linking up settlements. One such track went through Monyash and provided an alternative to the Derby to Manchester route. This track joined up several of the upland Peak District villages, passing close to Grangemill, then Elton, Middleton by Youlgreave, Monyash, Flagg and Chelmorton and then on to Dove Holes (but avoiding Buxton) (see Figure 19). This medieval route came down Derby Lane (now a green lane), past the guide stone (see Chapter 17) in to Monyash then off towards Flagg, via a track now called Cross Lane and past Knotlow Farm. Another route out of Monyash went from Monyash to Ashford along Horse Lane. There was also presumably a track, or just a path, from Monyash to Bakewell.

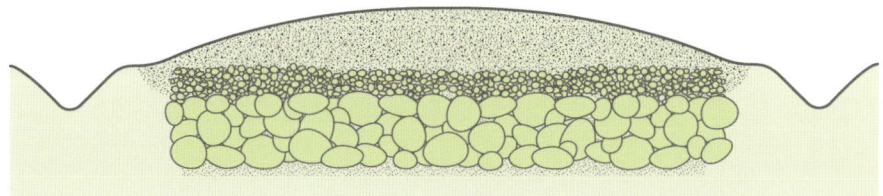

**Figure 18
Cross section
of a Roman
road**

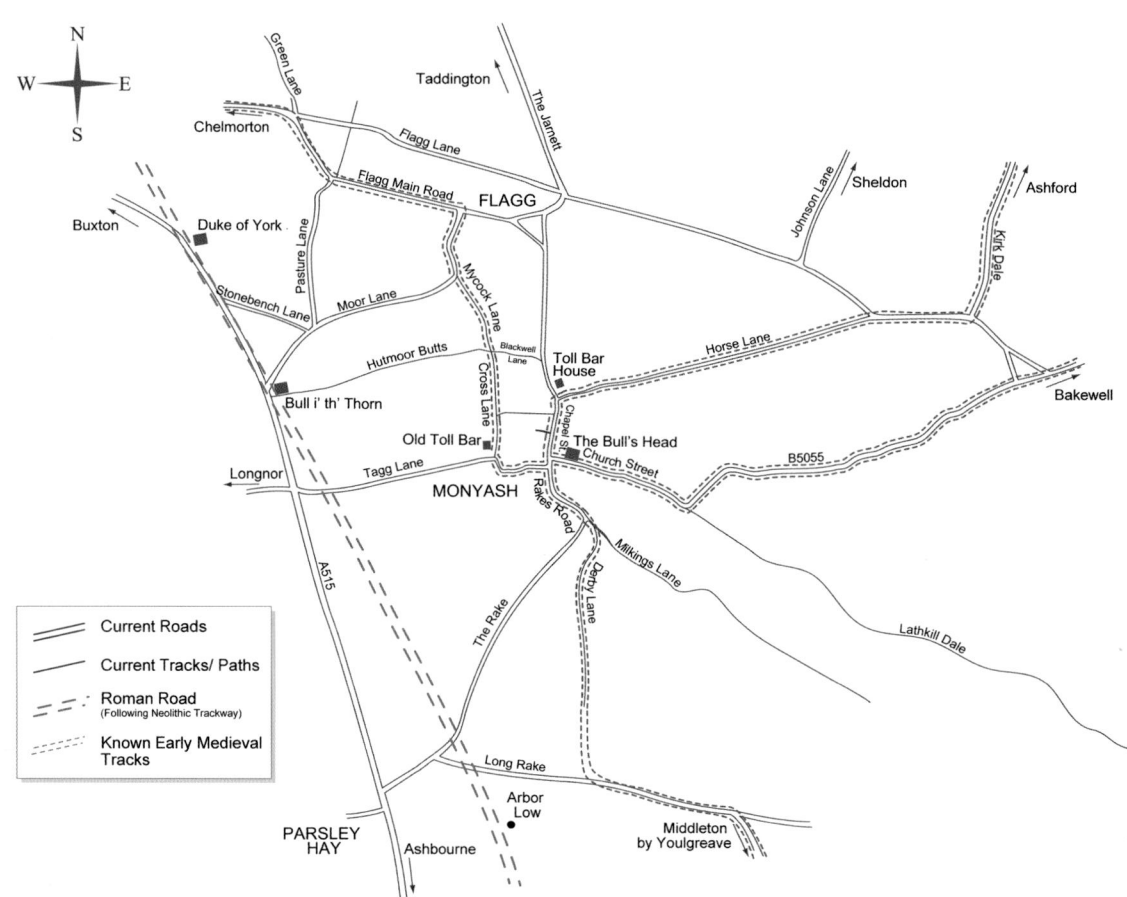

Figure 19 The Roman road and known Early Medieval tracks through Monyash

9. THE ARRIVAL OF CHRISTIANITY

During the Roman occupation of Britain another, though very different and less confrontational, invasion was underway. Christianity appears to have been well established in Britain by the 2nd century AD (see Box 8: Christianity). Over the next 400 years Anglo-Saxon kings were targeted and converted to Christianity. The Mercian king, Penda, who died in 655, was converted to Christianity in 653 and the first bishop of Mercia was Chad at Lichfield in AD 669. The kings then forced their subjects to accept Christianity, sometimes baptising them *en masse*, probably without their having much understanding of what they were doing. Pagan sites were adopted for Christian worship, so helping 'encourage' the conversion of the people who used them.

Importantly the Church and Christianity was the only real force that was tying together the various Anglo-Saxon kingdoms, unlike the raiding Vikings who were trying to tear them apart (see Box 9: Anglo-Saxon England). The Church provided an important base for education, learning and literacy. Bishops and monks, such as Bede (a renowned monk from Northumbria), played an important role in secular society as most kings could not read or write. They maintained land charters, documenting who owned what, and advised the kings on matters of state, in return for financial support for their monasteries and churches.

A Mercian royal monastery was established in Repton in the late 7th century and was the original seat of Christianity in this region, though the Mercian see (the Bishop's location or seat) was based in Lichfield. Many Mercian kings were buried in Repton.

During this time simple churches were built in towns and villages across the land. Around AD 920 a stone Anglo-Saxon church with ornate carvings was built in Bakewell. The inhabitants of Monyash would have travelled there for services until they were allowed to build their own church sometime around AD 1100 (see Box 13: Monyash Church 1100-1600).

Box 8: Christianity

Christianity began in the eastern Mediterranean in the mid-first century AD and arrived in Britain during the 2nd century AD, though its followers and missionaries were the subject of persecution for many years. In the 5th century St Patrick, a native of western Britain, converted much of the northern half of Ireland. Many monasteries were founded in Britain in the 6th century during a wave of religious enthusiasm. In AD 563 Saint Columba came from Ireland and introduced Christianity to parts of Scotland. In AD 597 Augustine, a senior member of a Benedictine monastery in Rome, was the first of many missionaries sent by Pope Gregory to convert the pagan Anglo-Saxons.[78] Out of the seven kings ruling the lands south of the Humber, including Ceawlin, King of Wessex, Augustine picked out Æthelberht, King of East Kent, whose seat was in Canterbury. Kent was likely chosen for two reasons; first, its closeness to mainland Europe and secondly, and importantly, Æthelberht had married Bertha, a Frankish Christian princess and daughter of the King of Paris. Thus Æthelberht became the first Anglo-Saxon king to convert to Christianity. He gave land in Canterbury for the building of the first Anglo-Saxon church, establishing the foundation of the Roman Church in England. (This would, 930 years later, become the home of the Church of England during the Reformation when Henry VIII created the Church of England, with himself as supreme head, breaking the churches in England away from the authority of the Pope.) Augustine became the first Archbishop of Canterbury. He died on the 26th May 604, and was later canonised St. Augustine of Canterbury.

Although based on the Roman Christian ethos, the British Church developed its own form of Christianity influenced by Columba and some existing Early British customs.[79] While the British and Roman Churches were not incompatible, there were important differences. The British Church was loosely structured and organised, based more on monastic life, whereas the Roman Church was highly structured and more disciplined. However there were three critical differences. Firstly, in the British tradition the king was all-powerful, whereas the head of the Roman Church was the Pope. Secondly, their monks had different forms of tonsure (haircut). And thirdly, they celebrated the most important day in the religious calendar, Easter, on different days. This created a particular problem for King Oswiu of Northumbria. (Oswiu was king of the Bernicians and defeated and killed Penda, King of Mercia, in 655 to become Bretwalda.) His second queen, Eanfled, was a devout Roman Christian. Due to the differences in the calculation of Easter, it was possible for there to exist a situation where, in some years, Oswiu would be celebrating Easter at the same time that his queen was still fasting in Lent. The next occasion when this would happen was going to be AD 665 and that might explain why a Synod of bishops was called in 664 to resolve some of the differences.[80]

Following the meeting of the Synod in Whitby in 664, the Roman style of worship, rules and practices were agreed upon including the Roman method for calculating Easter (see below). However, it would take another 300 years before the supremacy of the Roman Church was established over the British Church. Easter Sunday became the first Sunday after the 14th day of the lunar month. The calculation for the date of Easter is far from straightforward. (The precise computation and the results can be found in the tables provided in http://en.wikipedia.org/wiki/Computus.) Indeed, Easter may lie on any of the 35 possible dates between and including 22nd March and 25th April. It will next fall on 22nd March in 2160 and 25th April in 2038. The cycle of Easter dates repeats after exactly 5,700,000 years.

Some people have suggested ignoring the cycle of the moon and fixing Easter as the second Sunday in April. This suggestion has met with some limited support. Interestingly the Easter Act of 1928 set out legislation in the UK to allow the date of Easter to be fixed as the first Sunday after the second Saturday in April, i.e. the Sunday falling in the week of 9th April. However, this legislation has never been implemented, although it remains on the Statute book and could be implemented subject to approval by the various Christian Churches.[81] Agreement, however, seems unlikely.

Box 9: Anglo-Saxon England

The term Anglo-Saxon is often used to refer to the people of England and their culture from around AD 400 until the Norman conquest in 1066, though the first Anglo-Saxon king, Athelstan, did not rule until 924. The Anglo-Saxons knew themselves as the 'Englisc', from which the word 'English' derives. Their language was Anglo-Saxon or Old English.[82]

During the period from the 4th to 11th centuries the population was subject to attacks on many occasions as invaders tried to take control of Britain. The invaders included Picts (from Scotland), Angles, Saxons, Jutes (from around Germany, Denmark and the Netherlands), Vikings (from Norway and Denmark) and eventually the Normans (from Northern France who were themselves descended from earlier Viking invaders and the local population. Indeed, the word 'Norman' derives from 'Norse Men').

In AD 367 there was one particularly violent and co-ordinated raid by the Picts, Angles and Saxons. Towns were sacked and burned and many people killed. It took nearly two years for the Romans to restore some semblance of law and order. However at the start of the 5th century, with no Roman support, the invaders returned. Indeed requests were made to the Roman Emperor Honorius to return troops to Britain to help defend it against the invading armies. He, however, had greater problems at home; Rome had been sacked and the capital had moved temporarily to Ravenna. It was there he is reputed to have written to leading citizens of Britain explaining they would have to defend themselves from now on.

Despite these frequent attacks, much of the life in the countryside, particularly in the more remote areas, may have continued much as before, in particular in the Peak District where, for the first few hundred years at least, the invaders made little headway.

By the 7th century Britain was divided into many small and large Anglo-Saxon kingdoms. The Pecsætan (peaklanders) inhabited the central and northern parts of the Peak District and Monyash was in their territory. Sometime during the 7th century, the Pecsæte were annexed by Mercia becoming part of the northern division of Mercia (see Figure 15). Mercia was one of the most powerful kingdoms in England. Several of its kings, including Penda (who reigned from 626 to 655), Wulfhere (son of Penda who ruled 658-675), Æthelbald (who reigned from 716 until 757) and Offa (ruling from 757 to 796), held the position of overlord or Bretwalda over other Anglo-Saxon kingdoms. By the end of Offa's reign Mercia had grown from being a confederation of people under Mercian lordship to a vast kingdom comprising most of England between the Thames and the Humber.[83]

Whilst the various kingdoms were involved in territorial fighting they also had to deal with waves of Viking raiders. Norway had little land suitable for cultivation, so some of its inhabitants turned to the sea. Viking raids began in England in 793 when they destroyed the church on Lindisfarne. The Vikings were not just preoccupied with raiding and invading, but were also keen to establish trading relationships. They would have traded cod (which they preserved by hanging them up in the dry, icy, Nordic wind) and animal skins and furs (taken from the Sami in Lapland as taxes) and traded them for woollens, wheat, tin, honey and silver.[84] Trade with the Vikings also linked England to a wider commercial network including the Frankish Kingdoms (covering much of western Europe), China and Persia.

Eventually the Viking invaders occupied much of England, brutally driving out Anglo-Saxons from great areas of the country, installing Danish settlers as they advanced. In response to the

Danish invasions, King Æthelred of Wessex (grandson of Egbert) and his brother Alfred (later to become King of Wessex himself after the death of his brother in 871) led several bloody battles against the invaders, with a mix of defeats and victories.

On taking up the throne in 871, with a much weakened army, Alfred (the Great) was forced to make peace with Ivar the Boneless, the leader of the Danish invaders. During this peace with Wessex, the Danes turned to the north and attacked Mercia in a campaign that lasted until 874. The Danish leader, Ivar, died during this campaign and the Mercian leader, King Burgred (Offa's heir), was driven across the sea to Rome. Ivar was succeeded by Guthrum the Old, who finished the campaign against Mercia. In about 877 the Anglo-Saxon town near the Roman town of Little Chester was taken by the Danes and renamed Derby. (This name was a corruption of either the Danish and Gaelic *Djúra-bý* meaning Village or Farm of the Deer or its Roman name Derventio.[85]) In Mercia, the Danes appointed Coelwulf II, a Mercian, as the Viking's puppet ruler.[86] The Danes now had control over East Anglia, Northumbria and Mercia. This left Alfred as the only Anglo-Saxon king in England.

Guthrum nearly succeeded in conquering Wessex but he was defeated by Alfred at the Battle of Edington in 878. Alfred insisted that Guthrum was baptised and adopted the name Athelstan with Alfred as his godfather. A 'peace treaty' of 884 then set up the boundaries (partly based on Roman roads) for the area of Danish self-rule (The Danelaw) confining the Danes to the area north of a line drawn between London and Chester, including the kingdoms of Northumbria and East Anglia and the five boroughs of Derby, Leicester, Lincoln, Nottingham and Stamford.

Parts of England were now ruled by the Vikings whilst others were ruled by the Saxons. However battles continued, led by Alfred, as his army was the only major Saxon force left. When Alfred the Great died in 899, his successors extended their power northwards taking back areas from Danelaw. In AD 917 the Danes were expelled from Derby and a network of fortified burghs was created including, in 920, one at Bakewell. By 917 Edward the Elder (Alfred's son) was King of Mercia and Wessex. In 920 he became supreme lord of Northumbria but power alternated between English and the Danish (Viking) kings for the next 35 years. Athelstan, son of Edward the Elder and grandson of Alfred the Great, continued his father's expansionist policies, becoming the first King of (all) England in 927.[87] The last Viking king was Eric Bloodaxe who was killed in 954.[88]

However, the Danes did not give up their ambitions on England. England was subject to continuing raids into the 11th century, with short periods of stability and considerable bloodshed, with the crown moving between the English and Viking kings. Indeed there were fifteen different kings in the period between 900 and 1066.[89] Ironically, under the prosperity of Danelaw, Danish Jórvík, modern-day York, became a target for Viking raiders too.

In 1066, two rival 'Viking' factions led invasions of England. One under Harald Hardrada took York, but was defeated at the Battle of Stamford Bridge. The other, William, Duke of Normandy and his Norman army, defeated the Anglo-Saxon armies killing King Harold at the Battle of Hastings. (William was the great-great-great grandson of Rollo, a Viking Chieftain who conquered land in France in AD 911. William used boats for the invasion of England which were of the same type that the Vikings had used in their raids on England.[90])

King Harold II (Harold Godwinson 1022-1066) was not directly in line for the throne though his father was the powerful Earl of Wessex, a title Harold inherited in 1053. However he was the brother of King Edward the Confessor's wife, Edith. Harold was a highly-regarded fighter and army commander. With his armies he subjugated Wales in 1063 and negotiated an agreement with the Northumbrians. He also married twice, to high ranking Danish women. He became King after some confusion at the deathbed of the childless King of England, Edward the Confessor, in January 1066. Edward is reputed to have pointed to Harold as his successor. His natural heir, his great nephew, Edgar 'the Ætheling',[91] was just 15 years old and considered to be too young to rule and defend the country. However, there is little doubt that Edward had already promised the crown to William, who was loosely related to him. (Edward's maternal uncle was William's grandfather.) Further, William claimed that Harold had pledged allegiance to him in 1064. However, Harold was elected king by the Witenagemot (the assembly of important noblemen) and was crowned, in unseemly haste, in Westminster Abbey; the first king to be crowned there.

On hearing this William prepared his army for the invasion. Harold reigned for the short time until his death, on the 14th October 1066 at the Battle of Hastings, along with thousands of English and Norman troops. Edgar was then proclaimed king, but never crowned. He submitted to William a few weeks later.

The Saxon and Norman blood lines were later fused in 1100 when William's fourth son, Henry, married Edith (who changed her name to Matilda on becoming Queen). Edith was a descendant of Alfred the Great, the niece of Edgar and also daughter of King Malcolm III of Scotland. Henry I, an ancestor of Elizabeth II, ruled from August 1100 to December 1135.[92]

10. MONYASH – THE EARLIEST RECORD

After the Battle of Hastings in 1066, William, Duke of Normandy, now William I of England (often referred to as William the Conqueror) took control of Anglo-Saxon England. The earliest written record of Monyash is to be found at this time in the Domesday Book of 1086. This was William's audit of the country to find out who owned what (see Box 10: Norman England and the Domesday Book).

The Domesday Survey of Bakewell informs us that the Manor of Monyash was owned by the King with the exception of three carucates (about 360 acres) belonging to the Church and 16 acres in the hands of Henry de Ferrers. Henry de Ferrers, or more correctly Henri de Ferrières, was a Norman soldier who fought at the Battle of Hastings and was rewarded for his service with 210 manors throughout England, 114 of which were in Derbyshire. As a result he controlled much of south Derbyshire including the Royal Forest to the east (see Chapter 11) and the White Peak areas to the west of Monyash.

This Anglo-Norman ruler/administrator was also appointed as a legatus (commissioner/compiler) in the West Midlands area for the Domesday Survey. (His son, Robert de Ferrers (1062-1139), inherited his father's estates around 1100 AD, by which time they included land in Berkshire, Essex, Gloucester and Warwickshire. He bought the lead-rich estate of Wirksworth and, following his involvement in the Battle of the Standard against the Scots, King Stephen created him Earl of Derby.)

Monyash was referred to as Maneis in the Domesday Book (see Box 11: Monyash and the Domesday Book). Maneis was one of eight berewicks (outlying manorial dependencies belonging to the Lord of the Manor) of Bakewell. (A copy of the original page of the Domesday Book, with Bakewell and Monyash mentioned, is shown in Figure 20. Figure 21 provides an enlargement of the paragraph. A translation of the entry can be found in Box 11: Monyash and the Domesday Book). Bakewell, known at the time as the Royal Manor of Badeqvella (also sometimes Badecanwylla) which translates as Badecca's Well or Bath Well, was an important Anglo-Saxon ecclesiastical and royal administrative centre, with one of the few churches in the area.

There are no records of the size of the population of Monyash in 1086, but it most likely included a small number of farmers with large farms (50-100 acres/20-40 hectares), a few smallholders and some peasants with no land at all. Living would have been simple and frugal and relied upon farming, probably cows and sheep, and smallholdings for vegetables. Some people may have worked in a lead mine, possibly Mandale Mine, and others possibly doing small-scale 'mining' for lead around the village. Houses would have been made of wood, maybe some of wood and stone. The Domesday Book makes no mention of a church so the villagers would have travelled to Bakewell for services, possibly twice a week.

Box 10: Norman England and the Domesday Book

Compiling the Domesday Book (sometimes referred to as the Book of Reckoning) (1085-86) must have been a huge task since most people in the country were involved in some way or other. However, the Domesday Book was much more than a glorified audit; it was an attempt to control and subjugate the English aristocracy and landowners. The Normans had two related problems, rebellious landowners and the need to raise armies (from the rebellious landowners) to repel foreign invading armies.[93]

In return for their involvement in the conquest of England, William's knights were rewarded with land where they began pushing out the old ruling aristocracy and also the Church. Although the local lords and bishops had right of appeal against the land seizures, their complaints were heard by the sheriff, who was invariably in the pay of the new masters. Local rebellions were common and even Harold II's sons made two abortive attempts to recapture the country in 1068.

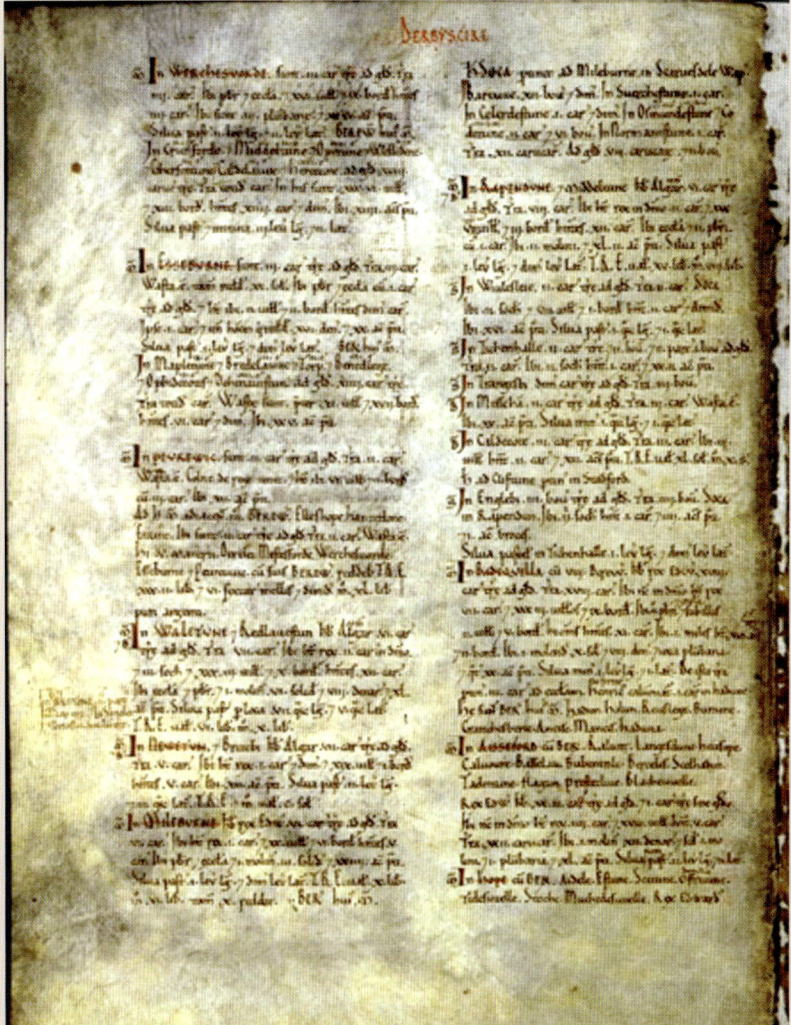

Figure 20 The page in the Domesday Book covering the Bakewell area

At the same time the Vikings continued their bloody raids on England. Around 1070 the King of Scotland and the King of Denmark joined forces to surprise, and then massacre, the occupants of the Norman garrison at Durham. Their armies then moved south and laid siege to York. Several earls saw this as an opportunity to rise up against their Norman oppressors. Soon the whole of northern Britain was in revolt.

William dealt with the problem with brutal efficiency, ransacking, burning and killing anything, innocent or guilty, that got in his way. On the way to York he built castles at Warwick and Nottingham. These were initially simple structures (motte-and-bailey – a stone or wooden structure on a raised earth mound surrounded by a ditch) which could be erected in just six days, but they formed easily defendable strongholds from which the Normans could exert control. His acts were so devastating that not only was there huge loss of life, but his destruction of crops caused a famine in Yorkshire. Indeed he had salt spread on the land which stunted crop growth, affecting the land for over 100 years.

After driving back the Danes he subjugated the Northumbrians, who until then had resisted Norman rule, and went on, in 1072, to invade and defeat the Scots.

Further revolts by the earls were swiftly and brutally dealt with. William replaced many of the earls and senior clerics with his own appointments. The problem for the English was that they had no central figure to lead them and the fortifications built by the Normans (Norman castles) provided a form of defence and a symbol of authority that had not been seen before. William ordered many castles, including the White Tower, an original part of the Tower of London, to be built around the country to ensure continued dominance over the rebellious English.

By 1085 the Normans held many, though not all, of the senior positions in government and the Church. To make things even more difficult for the old aristocracy, William and his administration spoke Norman French.

The English and Norman administrative and government structures were similar – they both were influenced by the Vikings and Romans. William went on to develop the existing form of government by increasing the power of the shires, making them autonomous administrative regions with fixed meeting places at specific towns, reporting directly to the King.

The Domesday Survey was William's audit of the country; a catalogue of who owned what and how much money he was due in taxes so he could ensure he had the means to raise armies to combat the continuing aggressive invasions of the Vikings. Tax was assessed and collected from the shires on behalf of the King by royal officers called the shire reeves (sheriffs), with individual reeves looking after each hundred.[94] Although not completed until the last year of William's life, the Domesday Book is Britain's earliest public record.[95]

The Domesday Book comprises two handwritten volumes. One, known as Little Domesday, covered Essex, Norfolk and Suffolk. Though this was the larger volume of the two, the second is known as the Great Domesday. This covered the rest of England, though in much less detail than the Little Domesday book, excluding areas that were as yet not controlled by William (parts of Cumbria and Northumbria). Also, there were no surveys conducted in some of the larger towns, such as London, presumably due to the size and difficulty of getting the information.

Box 11: Monyash and the Domesday Book

The entry for the Bakewell area, including Monyash, in the Domesday Book can be translated as follows:[96]

In Bakewell with eight berewicks (outlying dependencies, demesne farms, belonging to the Lord of the Manor), King Edward had 18 carucates* of land taxable - land for 18 plough teams. There now the King has in lordship seven carucates, and 33 villagers and nine bordars (smallholders). There are two priests and a church, and under them two villagers and five smallholders. All these have 11 ploughs (between them). One knight has 16 acres of land and two smallholders. There is a mill (probably a corn mill) worth 10 shillings and 8 pence (53p), and one lead mine (possibly Mandale Mine), 80 acres of meadow and woodland at least three miles long and three miles wide. Three carucates of that land belong to the Church. Henry de Ferrar (de Ferrers) claims one carucate in Hadune (Haddon or Over Haddon). The berewicks of the manor are: Hadun (Haddon), Holun (Holme in Bakewell), Reuslege (Rowsley), Burtune (Burton in Bakewell), Cranchesberie (Conksbury), Aneise (One Ash), Maneis (Monyash), Hadun (Over Haddon).**

* A carucate (a subdivision of a wapentake – the Danish equivalent of a Hundred) was a term used in the areas that had been subject to Danelaw. One carucate was roughly the area an eight oxen plough team could plough in a year, nominally 120 acres (49 hectares). Carucates would vary in size since a plough team would be able to plough less land if the soil was poor or the ground uneven. However each carucate remained fixed over time providing a stable base for tax assessment purposes.

** The settlements of Conksbury and Haddon, or Nether Haddon, were abandoned at some point after 1086. Conksbury lay just west of Conksbury Bridge and the outline of the houses and tracks of Nether Haddon are visible in the fields near Haddon Hall. Its church now forms part of the chapel of Haddon Hall.[97]

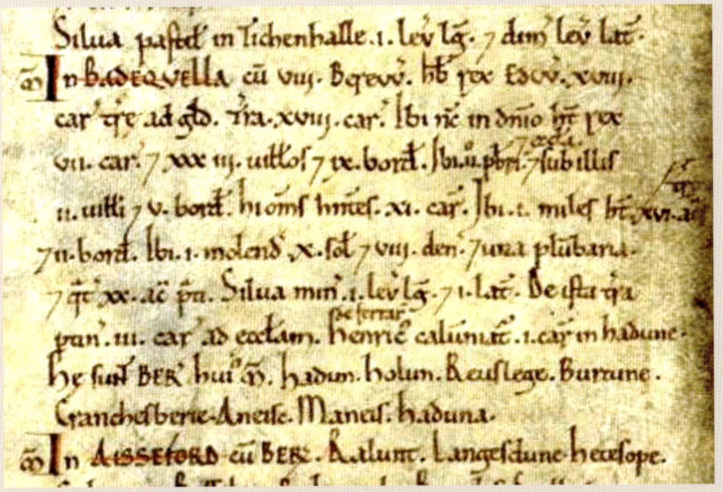

Figure 21 Section of the Domesday Book showing Maneis

Maneis (Monyash) is in the second line up from the bottom.

11. MONYASH AFTER THE CONQUEST

King William was a lover of hunting and he established huge areas of 'Royal Forest' – areas set aside for the King and aristocracy to pursue their pastime. A 'forest' was not necessarily an area of woodland but any large area of heath or grassland that supported game. In the 12th century one third of England was designated as Royal Forest and protected by 'Forest Laws'. The strict controls of these lands, which were relaxed in the mid to late 13th century and slowly fell out of use, were highly unpopular as they made it difficult for some inhabitants to farm the land as they used to. Parts of Derbyshire became two such royal playgrounds.

The Forest of the High Peak comprised the large area of moorland covering much of Derbyshire north of Buxton and Tideswell (north of Monyash) under the control of William Peverel. Peverel (or Peveril) built what is now known as Peveril Castle above Castleton. Initially a wooden fortified home, it was used to enforce Norman rule and control lead mining in the area. All this land eventually became part of the Duchy of Lancaster and then leased, in perpetuity, to the Dukes of Devonshire.[98]

The area to the east of the River Derwent, east of a line from Castleton through Matlock, later became the Forest of East Derbyshire. This was relatively open country surrounded by a wall to keep out sheep and cattle from the 'game reserve', and under the control of Henry de Ferrers (Henry de Ferrar in the Domesday Book). It is believed that de Ferrers built a motte-and-bailey castle at Pilsbury, three miles south west of Monyash. This 'castle' was a fenced enclosure, in fact two enclosures, on two outcrops of rock separated by a deep ditch from where he controlled the area.[99]

Monyash was just outside the Royal Forest; the whole of the limestone plateau/White Peak area, now devoid of much tree cover, was of little interest to the nobility. At the time of the Domesday Book, parts of Monyash were in the hands of Henry de Ferrers. At some time between 1100 and 1135, land in Monyash was given to William Peverel. The inhabitants of Monyash continued farming and tried to ride out the many changes in ownership (lords of the manor) that followed and the lengthy legal disputes resulting from those changes (see Box 12: Lords of the Manor of Monyash 1066-1721).

Box 12: Lords of the Manor of Monyash 1066-1721

Whoever thought they owned land in England, whether they were the Anglo-Saxon aristocracy, the Church or freeholders, were in for a shock in 1066 when King William declared that all the land was his. Based on the Norman 'feudal' system the King then gave land to the people who had served him well in war and to his key supporters, usually appointing them as nobles, such as lords and knights. Some land was also given to the Church, again usually to his supporters. By 1087 only eight per cent of the land was held by Anglo-Saxon knights and barons.[100]

For the peasant farmers it meant little change. They continued to work the land for their new masters and possibly also pay tithes, equivalent to ten per cent of their outputs, to the Church (*tithe is derived from the Old English for tenth*).

Some time before 1086, William had given some of Monyash, and parts of Derbyshire, Staffordshire and Leicestershire, to a Norman soldier, Henry de Ferrers, (Henri de Ferrières) for his service during the Battle of Hastings.

(Note: From this point forward the ownership of Monyash becomes difficult to follow. Multiple 'owners' are mentioned and it is not possible to separate out precisely who owned what lands, churches or tithes.)

King William died in 1087 at the age of 62 and was succeeded briefly by his son William II. Following a fatal hunting accident in the New Forest in 1100, his brother, Henry, came to the throne. During the reign of King Henry I (1100-1135) the manor of Bakewell, including Monyash, was put in the hands of William Peverel (rumoured to have been an illegitimate son of William I).

When Peverel died in 1113 his land (demesne farms) in Monyash as well as vast amounts of land and many churches (and their incomes) in many counties, including Derbyshire, Leicestershire, Nottinghamshire and Buckinghamshire were given to Lenton Abbey, which Peverel founded. (There is some doubt about the legitimacy of this record as it was witnessed by Gerard, Archbishop of York, who died in 1108.)[101]

Henry had no male heirs so, before his death, he persuaded his barons to swear allegiance to his daughter Matilda, his only surviving child. The barons were not persuaded and she was forced to step aside in favour of Henry's nephew, Stephen of Blois (and grandson of William the Conqueror) who then ruled England from 1135 to 1154. However this led to a civil war between Stephen's supporters and Matilda, resolved only on Stephen's death when Matilda's son, Henry II, took the throne.[102]

Henry II then confiscated a great deal of land and their associated tithes, in particular those in the Peak District, including Monyash and Bakewell and its associated chapelries. Henry then gave them to his second son, John, Count of Mortain. (Other sources suggest that these lands were given to John later, around 1194, by his older brother when he became Richard I.)

Henry was succeeded by his son, Richard, in 1189. However Richard I (the Lion Heart) spent little time in England and much time fighting, mainly against Muslims, in the Holy Land during the Crusades. Rather than appoint John as ruler of England in his absence, King Richard appointed William de Longchamps, his Chancellor and also Bishop of Ely, as Chief Justiciar (a sort of Prime minister) to manage the country. John was not seen as reliable. Indeed the childless Richard had even refused to recognise his brother as heir to the throne. John took his brother's absence as an opportunity to get rid of Longchamps. With the help of Hugh de Nonant (or Hugh de Novant), Bishop of Coventry and Lichfield (which also covered Derbyshire and Warwickshire) and a close political advisor, they led a campaign against Longchamps and succeeded in forcing Longchamps to relinquish his power in 1191. [103]

As a reward for his services John gave Nonant three sheriffdoms (which as a Bishop he was not allowed to hold) and also the churches of Bakewell and Hope, along with the income from their lands and associated churches, including Monyash Church. Nonant took the income from the lands for himself leaving the churches in a dire financial position.

Richard returned to England in 1194. John surrendered to him in Nottingham after trying to prevent his return. Richard forgave John and named him as his heir. Nonant was less fortunate and had to relinquish his ill-gotten gains and pay a substantial fine. Shortly afterwards he retired to Normandy. John became King on the death of Richard in battle in 1199.

John confirmed the gift of the lands and churches to Nonant's successor, Geoffrey Muschamp. Later Muschamp's successors, William de Cornhill (1215-1224) and/or Alexander Stavenby (1224-1240) transferred these rights to the Dean and Chapter of Lichfield. Almost immediately a protracted legal dispute began which lasted nearly 300 years, during which period there were several appeals to the Ecclesiastical court. The key issues were the rights of William Peverel to acquire the land, the ability to bequeath tithes for land not under cultivation at the time of the bequest, and the rights of sequestration of John, Count of Mortain. At times the dispute became violent and it was never fully resolved until the time of the Reformation when Henry VIII seized all Church property.[104]

While Monyash Church, some land and associated tithes moved between State and Church, other parts of Monyash were said to be held by Robert de Salocia and Matthew de Aston in 1199, William de Lynford until 1338, William de Lynford Jr. until 1349, then Sir Laurence de Lynford and, in 1364, his son William Lynford and John de Stafford.[105]

At some point Monyash, or at least parts of Monyash, appear to have been acquired by King Henry III who gave them (together with other land) to Eleanor of Provence. When she married him in 1236 the land conveniently reverted to the Crown. In 1549 or 1550 Monyash, or parts of it, were sold to Sir William Cavendish (whose descendants were later to become the Dukes of Devonshire). On his death his wife, Bess of Hardwick, married George Talbot, 6th Earl of Shrewsbury, in 1567. He died in 1590 and the manor of Monyash was inherited by his son Gilbert (his mother was Lady Gertrude Manners, George's first wife). The manor of Monyash was broken up after the death, in 1616, of Gilbert, 7th Earl of Shrewsbury (who married Bess of Hardwick's daughter), as he had no male heirs. His estate, including the manor of Monyash, was split three ways between his three daughters Mary, wife of William, Earl of Pembroke, Elizabeth, wife of Henry, Earl of Kent and Alathea, wife of Thomas, Earl of Arundel. The earldom passed to his younger brother, Edward.[106]

By 1640 Philip, Earl of Pembroke, owned two of the parts of the manor of Monyash. He then sold them to John Shallcross who, in 1646, resold them to Thomas Gladwin of Tupton Hall (one of the foremost lead merchants of the mid 17th century who had an estimated income of £1,000 per year and was worth £10,000).[107] His granddaughters passed the estate to Sir Talbot Clarke and Dr Henry Bourne. In 1721 Edward Cheney became the Lord of the Manor of Monyash when he purchased two thirds of the land from the then landowners Sir Talbot Clarke and Dr Henry Bourne and the final third, in 1735, from John Gilbert.[108] (For the next stage in Monyash's ownership see Box 18: The Cheney Family.)

12. MONYASH CHURCH – THE BEGINNINGS

It is possible that Monyash Church began as a simple wooden cross around which people gathered for worship, maybe where the Church stands today, which was probably the site of an even older pagan religious meeting place. (The yew tree by the south porch of the Church is said to be one of the oldest in the county and may even predate the church and could signify the location of an earlier religious site.)

Figure 22 The original Chapel in Monyash?

The original Anglo-Saxon chapel would have been a simple stone (or possibly wooden) building with a nave and chancel under one roof. It was likely constructed some time after the Domesday Survey of 1086 and before 1199 when there are the first records of a church in Monyash, though "there is little doubt that there had been a chapel there for some time" i.e. well before 1199.[109] (See Figure 22 for an impression of the original Church building and Box 13: Monyash Church 1100-1600.)

The Chapel was founded and controlled by its mother Church in Bakewell to minister to the needs of not only the villagers of Monyash but also the nearby villagers of Flagg, Hurdlow and One Ash.[110] It must have been some relief to the inhabitants not to have to attend church in Bakewell several times a week, especially during bad weather. However the villagers had to contribute both to the running of the Chapel in Monyash and also the Church in Bakewell, which they were expected to use for christenings, weddings and funerals, and also attend for the major feast days.

By 1199 the Chapel had been greatly extended eastwards, with a separate chancel which included a sedilia (see Figure 23 and Box 13: Monyash Church 1100-1600). The two lower stages of the tower were added around 1250 and it might have been topped with a small spire (though not the one we see today). Two local landowners were responsible for the developments and for donating land to provide an income to pay for a priest.[111]

It is likely that the Church was dedicated to St Leonard sometime between 1100 and the middle of the 13th century. St Leonard was a 6th century nobleman from Limoges who declined a bishopric and became a recluse in the forest of Limousin. He was reputedly rewarded by his godfather, King Clovis I, with all the land he could ride around on a donkey in a day in return for his prayers that had brought the Queen safely through a difficult childbirth. He founded the Abbey of Noblac, 21 kilometres from Limoges, on the land he was given, around which then grew the town of Saint-Léonard de Noblat. He died around AD 559 and his feast day is 6th November.[112] King William and his followers had a natural preference for 'French' Saints, but further, because of their love of hunting, they particularly admired Saints associated with forests. Leonard was also credited with miracles leading to the release of prisoners, which appealed to the Normans because they would often get themselves into violent scrapes and then needed to be bailed out.

Figure 23 The sedilia

Box 13: Monyash Church 1100-1600

Dominating the landscape, and visible for miles around, is St Leonard's Church which dates back to around, or even before, AD 1100. This medieval Church, with its large octagonal spire, is surprisingly large for such a small village and has an equally surprising history. It also contains many unusual and intriguing features. The building is a patchwork of additions and developments. The major enlargements took place around 1199, 1250, 1348 and 1370, followed by two major restorations in 1886-1888 (see Box 25: The Butterfield Restoration 1886-1888) and 1996-2006 (see Box 30: The 1996-2006 Restoration). Today the Church is a grade II* listed building of national importance.

Prior to the building of the Chapel in Monyash, villagers travelled to Bakewell, maybe twice a week, for services. The only churches around at this time were at Ashbourne, Bradbourne, Bakewell, Darley, Hope, Tideswell and Wirksworth before the spate of church building in late Norman times. Bakewell was a Saxon Royal Foundation Church and a Collegiate Church - a kind of team ministry responsible for the other congregations in the outlying villages. The Church played an important part in people's lives, collecting taxes, teaching them about Heaven and Hell and also providing a rudimentary education.

The original Church in Monyash was likely to have been a small (Anglo-Saxon) chapel, probably a simple stone building, dating back to sometime around 1100. During the 12th century the Normans and Norman architecture influenced the shape and style of the rapidly developing (and increasingly rich) churches across England. Churches became much larger and based on the shape of the cross (see Figure 24) often with areas separated out by screens. The windows would have been quite narrow since wider ones might not have been able to support the weight of the roof. Masonry work was relatively simple though archways were often decorated with carvings. Stone columns were used to support high wooden roofs. A lot of use was made of the rounded arch[113] though these have, in many churches including Monyash, been replaced by Gothic (pointed) arches.

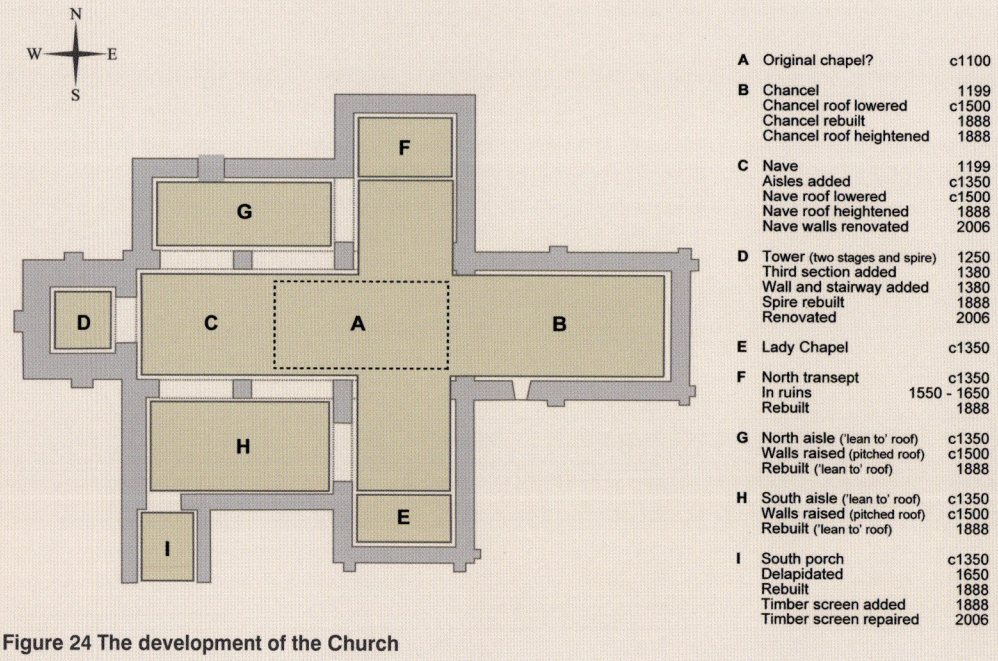

A	Original chapel?	c1100
B	Chancel	1199
	Chancel roof lowered	c1500
	Chancel rebuilt	1888
	Chancel roof heightened	1888
C	Nave	1199
	Aisles added	c1350
	Nave roof lowered	c1500
	Nave roof heightened	1888
	Nave walls renovated	2006
D	Tower (two stages and spire)	1250
	Third section added	1380
	Wall and stairway added	1380
	Spire rebuilt	1888
	Renovated	2006
E	Lady Chapel	c1350
F	North transept	c1350
	In ruins	1550 - 1650
	Rebuilt	1888
G	North aisle ('lean to' roof)	c1350
	Walls raised (pitched roof)	c1500
	Rebuilt ('lean to' roof)	1888
H	South aisle ('lean to' roof)	c1350
	Walls raised (pitched roof)	c1500
	Rebuilt ('lean to' roof)	1888
I	South porch	c1350
	Delapidated	1650
	Rebuilt	1888
	Timber screen added	1888
	Timber screen repaired	2006

Figure 24 The development of the Church

In 1199 two local landowners, Robert de Salocia and Matthew de Aston, who are thought to have been joint lords of the manor of Monyash, were responsible for the first major development of the Church in a Norman style. They were keen to demonstrate the village's (or more likely their own) wealth and ambitions. They provided the funds to enlarge the building and add a separate chancel (see Figure 24). They also provided Bakewell Church with the income from an oxgang of land (about eight hectares) together with a house in Monyash to provide funds for a chaplain to celebrate mass three times a week, on Sundays, Wednesdays and Fridays, in Monyash.[114] (The permission granted for this was the second written mention of the Church in Monyash).[115] In return for this the inhabitants of Monyash agreed that each house would provide a farthing a year (there were 960 farthings in a pound) to cover the cost of lighting the Chapel; this was in addition to the fees they already paid to Bakewell Church. They also agreed that they would attend the mother Church in Bakewell on All Saints' Day, and at Christmas and Easter.[116] The church in Bakewell retained its lucrative rights to christen and bury people.

On the arch between the chancel and the nave are two corbels sticking out from the pillars to support the arch, which were probably carved around this time. The corbels have carved faces with foliage above, though the foliage above the north side face was replaced around 1888 (see Figure 25 and Box 25: The Butterfield Restoration 1886-1888). There is also some evidence that there was a rood screen, a screen with a crucifix and maybe statues on it, separating the chancel from the nave. Within the chancel de Salocia and de Aston included a sedilia, a most unusual feature in a small country chapel. A sedilia is a set of three stone seats set into the stonework on the south side of a chancel for the use of the priest and his assistants (the deacon and the sub deacon) (see Figure 23). The seats are at different heights, depending on seniority, with the highest on the eastern side. There is often also an additional niche for a piscina (a shallow basin which used to be used for washing the communion vessels). This extension can be seen in the Monyash sedilia. The seats have rounded ('Norman' style) stone canopies with cylindrical shafts either side of the seats 'supporting' the canopy. During the Butterfield Restoration (see Box 25: The Butterfield Restoration 1886-1888) the original stone shafts were replaced with marble ones. More recently the original shafts were put back and the two marble shafts are currently standing at the back of the Church.

De Salocia and de Aston later paid for the construction of the two lower stages of the tower between 1225 and 1250. It is thought that the tower was topped by a small spire.[117]

It would appear that Bakewell Church and its associated chapels were not particularly affluent and struggled to cover their running costs, indeed many village priests were exceedingly poor.[118] There were regular disputes over the finances between Bakewell Church and the Dean and Chapter of Coventry and Lichfield Cathedral. As a result Monyash struggled to secure the income it was due from both Lichfield and Bakewell. In 1280 the Archbishop of Canterbury, Archbishop Peckham (or Pecham), visited Bakewell and discovered that the vicar and his team of assistant priests, the deacon and sub-deacon, were quite inadequately paid. He strongly criticised the Dean and Canons of Lichfield for their neglect of Bakewell Church and its associated chapels and insisted they increase their allowances.[119] (At this time the see of Coventry and Lichfield also covered Derbyshire and Warwickshire. In 1539 the name was reversed to become the Diocese of Lichfield and Coventry. In 1837 Coventry was transferred to the Diocese of Worcester and Lichfield became a separate diocese. In 1884 Derbyshire was united with the diocese of Lincoln to form the Diocese of Southwell. The diocese of Derby became independent in 1927.)

In a compromise agreement it was decided that the inhabitants of Monyash would maintain the chancel and supply a chalice (the cup used to hold wine during Mass) and missal (the service book) and provide an additional 13s 4d (66p) and twelve acres of land to support a priest. In return the

Figure 25 Norman carved faces. The left hand face is found in the sedilia and the other two are on the corbels supporting the chancel arch.

Cathedral chapter agreed to provide the rest of the priest's fee and all the books, robes and utensils required for the services and to maintain the rest of the building.[120]

This agreement did not appear to resolve the situation and it was not until 1315 that a more lasting settlement was reached between Lichfield and all the chapels of Bakewell. The Chapel of Monyash was supported with a grant of 15 shillings (75p) and was relieved of a number of costs including charges for maintenance of the buildings and the supply of holy water. However the villagers agreed to pay the usual tithes (on the sale of wool and lambs) to the Dean and Chapter of Lichfield (not to Lenton Priory – see Box 12: Lords of the Manor of Monyash 1066-1721). (This is rather different to the situation today when the Church of England makes no contribution towards the day-to-day expenses of its parish churches. Indeed the parish churches have to make a contribution towards the overheads of the Church and the Diocese in which they sit.)

Around the middle of the 14th century Monyash prospered with the growth of the lead mining industry and the granting of its own market. The Church also became richer. Churches extracted tithes from the inhabitants (ten per cent of income payable in cash or produce from the land) and income from taxes from lead mining (see Chapter 15: Monyash Mines and Quarries). Around this time it is believed that the nave was rebuilt and extended outwards, with columns and gothic arches to create north and south aisles with 'lean-to' roofs.[121] This development greatly increased the size of the Church. The square-headed windows with the ornate carvings (tracery) would have been added at this time (see Figure 26) adding to the feeling of space and light. The southern chancel Y-shaped tracery window (with many small panes) may have been fitted a little earlier, or moved from an earlier position during one of the many redevelopments.

In 1345 the Chapel also received burial rights which provided it with some useful additional income, though a proportion was taken by Bakewell and Lichfield (a farthing to the Vicar of Bakewell for each burial and an annual fee of 12 pence to the Dean and Chapter).[122]

On 3rd July 1348 Nicholas de Congesdon and his brother John, who may have been collectors of tithes of lead, hay and corn for the Church and also local landowners, further extended the Chapel and built the south transept to create a Chantry Chapel (which later became the Lady Chapel).[123] It is thought a north transept was added around this time, balancing the south transept/ Lady Chapel to complete the cruciform plan of the Church. The brothers also donated land in

Monyash, Sterndale and Chelmorton to cover the additional cost of a chantry priest to celebrate a daily service at Monyash in the Chantry Chapel.[124] (Chantry priests were ordained priests who performed a number of duties in the church including saying masses for the local nobility and often helping with the education of the poor.) From then until the Reformation in the 16th century, Monyash had two priests, one giving a daily mass and a second celebrating mass three times a week.

It is thought that the two transepts were initially closed off from the aisles, presumably by screens, as both of them contain piscinas, indicating that they both had altars. Some sources date the oak chest at the rear of the church to around the 14th century. It was likely used to hold the altar plate and priests vestments.[125]

Later in the 14th century, a third section was added to the tower. This section had battlements and the tower was topped by an octagonal spire (similar to the one we see today – it was rebuilt around 1888). A new west front was built on the south aisle to create a stairway between the old and new walls to provide an unusual access to the tower; a form of access which is probably unique amongst English parish churches.[126] It is believed that the south porch was also probably constructed around this time, built over a beautifully moulded doorway.

At this time, churches were not just used for services. They served as community centres and the porches were sometimes used as courts, in particular coroner's courts, where inquests were held for people who had been accidentally or wilfully killed.

Figure 26
Square-headed
window

Towards the end of the 15th century the walls of the nave were raised and the high pitch roof was lowered (as can be seen later in Figure 41) supported by Gothic arches (pointed arches rather than the rounded Norman arches). It is likely that three two-light clerestory windows (windows in the Church wall above the aisle roofs) were also added around this time.[127] The 15th century font, mentioned in Herald's Visitation of 1569, indicates that the Chapel had also acquired baptismal rights. (Heraldic Visitations were tours of inspection, started by Henry VIII, undertaken by the King of Arms, a senior ranking court official, in order to check that the nobles had the right 'to bear arms'. The nobility had to provide evidence that they had the right to a coat of arms and their titles.)

The Reformation during the reign of Henry VIII (1509-1547) and continued by his son Edward VI (1547-1553) was a difficult time for the Church. Following protracted disputes with the Pope and the Catholic Church in Rome, which began over his desire to have his marriage to Catherine of Aragon, widow of his brother Arthur, annulled, Henry split the English Church from the Roman Church and declared himself the supreme head of the Church of England. This view of the King having divine right to rule both the Church and the State was at odds with the Roman Church's view that the Pope was God's representative on Earth and should also have the ultimate authority over the state.

The substantial income previously paid to Rome was now paid to the King. It had also not escaped the King's notice that the Church owned between one-fifth and one-third of the land in all England. His chief minister, Thomas Cromwell, realised that he could ensure the gentry and nobility supported this new Royal Supremacy by selling them some of the Church lands.[128] Much Church property including monasteries (in what is known as the Dissolution of the Monasteries) was seized by the Crown and some of it sold on to the nobility. In a move that further upset many of the ordinary working people Henry also abolished many feast days, some of the few occasions when people could enjoy time off and celebrate something. This land seizure also resulted in the loss of the chantry priests, who were paid for by the return on land given to the Church, and this too had an effect on local communities as chantry priests often acted as schoolmasters.[129] The chantry land in Monyash was seized by the Crown (see Box 12: Lords of the Manor of Monyash 1066-1721) and as a result the chantry priest, Michael Bredwell (or Bredewell) (a former canon) was pensioned off in 1548, despite the custom that a chantry priest held his position for life or until he chose to give it up.

13. INCREASING PROSPERITY

In the 13th century Monyash would have comprised a scattering of small cottages and farms roughly where some of them stand today. Around the centre of the village would have been many small fields enclosed by dry stone walls. Beyond this was common or waste land used by sheep and also for turbary (see Figure 27). Turbary was the right of villagers to dig turf for fuel. However, as this land lay between several villages there were frequent disputes. In 1278 a jury was commissioned to inquire into the activities of Ralph de Wyne (or Ralph le Wyne) and other Monyash men who were accused of trying to prevent the men of Taddington, Priestcliffe, Ashford and Sheldon from "exercising their ancient right to dig turf and gather heath in the Marshes of Monyash".[130] Their turf stacks had been cut into small pieces during the night and the heath stolen. (This may also have been a dispute over the ownership of the more valuable lead in the area, see Chapter 15.[131]) In 1586 and 1590 two more disputes between the men of Monyash and the men of Over Haddon reached the High Court. It was not until the common and waste lands were enclosed in the 1770s (see Chapter 23) that these problems finally ended. [132]

Many of the trackways in Monyash, as in the rest of the country, were in some state of disrepair and a law, passed in 1285, made their upkeep the responsibility of the landowners. (Indeed the upkeep of roads was a major problem right up until recent times; some would say it still is.) Any changes in the routes also required a licence to be obtained from the King.

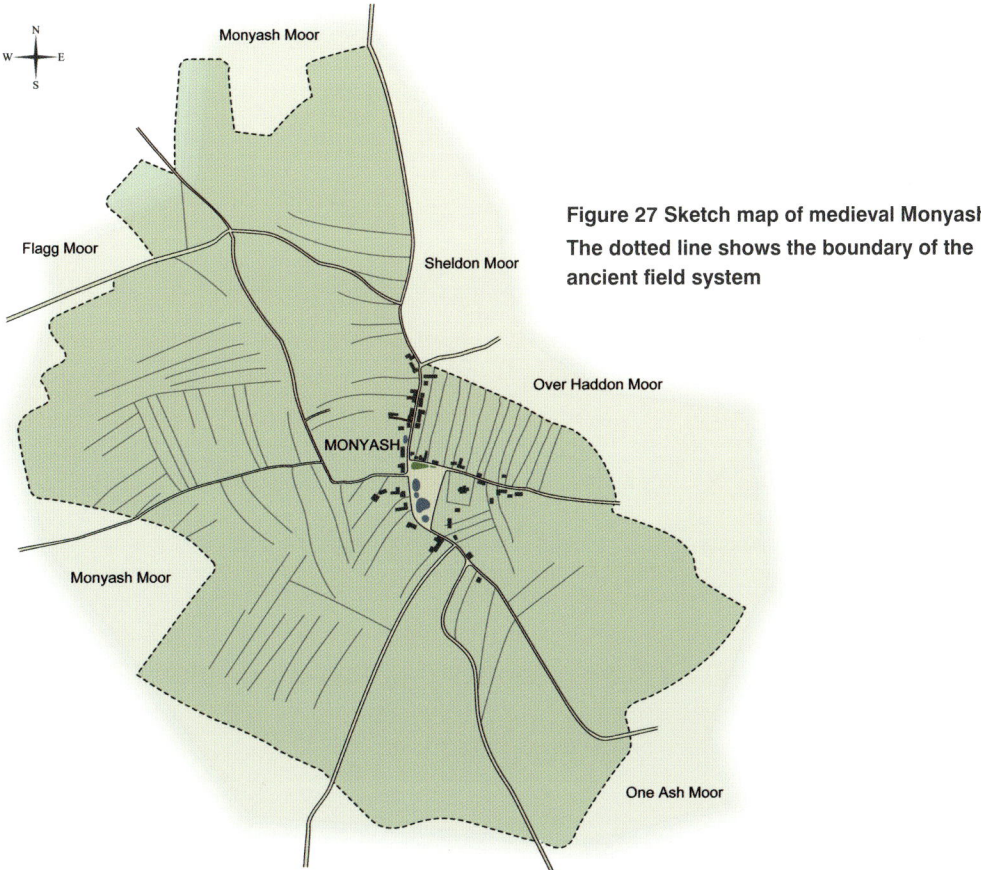

Figure 27 Sketch map of medieval Monyash
The dotted line shows the boundary of the
ancient field system

Close to Monyash the old Roman road from Derby to Manchester was still in existence though it may have been falling into disuse in favour of the smaller tracks linking towns and villages. Monyash was also at the crossroads of several trackways (see Box 15: Packhorse Ways, Saltways and Drovers' Roads) including:

- the 'alternative' route from Derby to Manchester passing through many villages,
- the saltway from Cheshire to Bakewell and beyond,
- a drovers' road from the west of the country to Ashford and beyond, and
- another drovers' road to Tideswell and Peak Forest and beyond (see Figure 28).

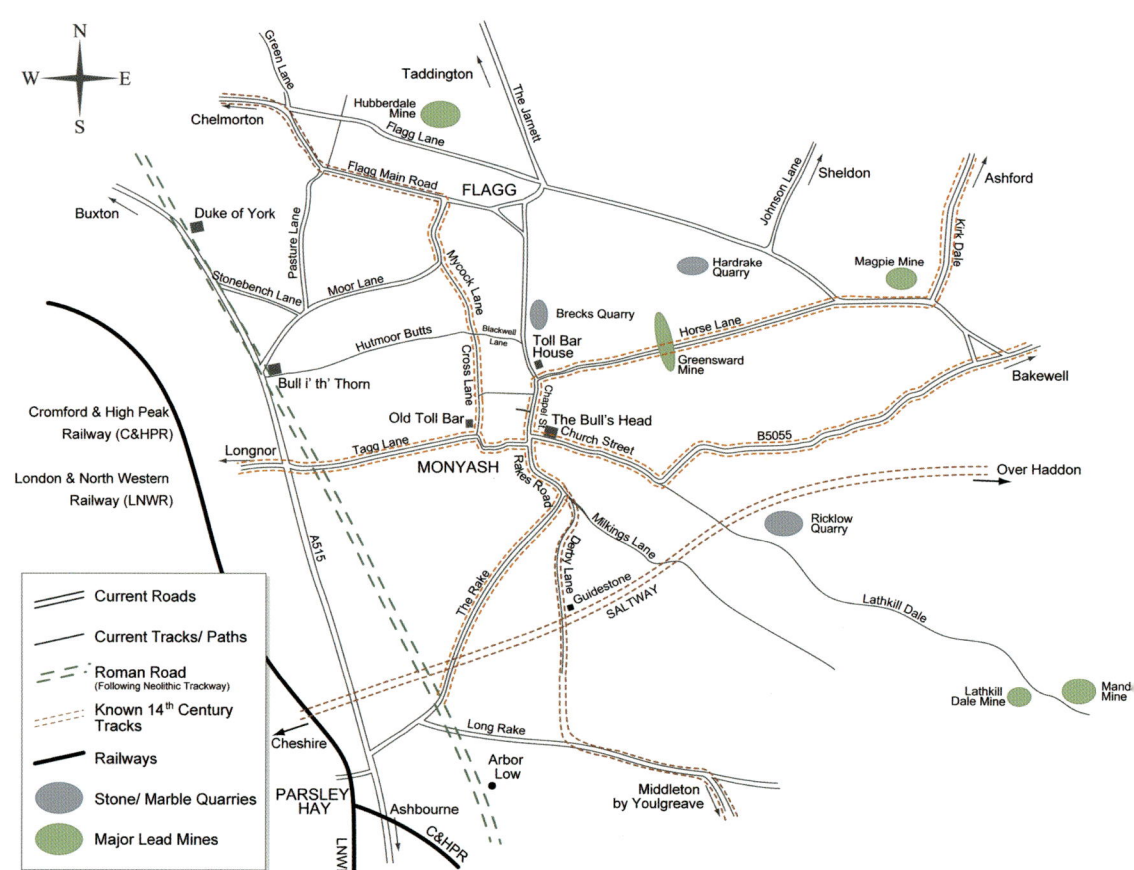

Figure 28 Major quarries, 14th century tracks and the 19th century railways

Only one of these routes is a main road today (Tagg Lane from the Longnor direction). The other routes were Derby Lane (now a green lane), Cross Lane via Knotlow Farm to Flagg (now a small track) and the road to Ashford (now Horse Lane, a single track road within a wide green lane).

These tracks in and around Monyash became even more important to the livelihood of the villagers after the granting of the charter for a market in 1340. Keeping the tracks in good condition encouraged people to visit the market, trade and spend money. Even if the tracks were in good condition people would only have travelled from about seven miles away, which gave them just enough time to get there and back home in a day as well as spend time at the market.

The charter was granted on 8th April 1340. From then on Monyash was entitled to hold a weekly market every Tuesday and a three day annual fair shortly after Whitsun (seven weeks after Easter). Monyash was one of the villages to receive such a charter quite late; one of the earliest was Hartington in 1203. Bakewell was granted one in 1254 followed by Ashbourne in 1257. Monyash's market charter was witnessed by the Archbishop of Canterbury, the Bishops of Durham and Lincoln and the Earls of Surrey and Derby.[133] It is likely that the original market cross was erected at this time on the village green, where the markets used to take place. The base of this cross is still visible beneath a more recently added pillar. It is reputed that a set of stocks stood on this base before the current pillar was erected.

Records show that the fairs and markets had been discontinued by 1811, though they may well have ended many years before then.[134] By 1845 the fairs and markets appear to have been re-established; the market on Thursday and four fairs (the Saturday before the 2nd Tuesday in February, 14th May, the Monday before the 2nd Wednesday in September and 19th October). In 1881 the weekly market had moved back to Tuesdays and a three day fair was held again around Whitsun. By 1899 the market and fairs had again died out though a small travelling fair continued to visit occasionally. In 1965 a small market and fair was revived on the May (Spring) and August bank holidays to raise money for a village in India (see Figure 29).[135] The market/fair on the May bank holiday Monday continues to this day and is used to raise money for local and national causes.

Figure 29 The fair circa 1965
A travelling fair being erected in the grounds of Monyash House Farm.

14. GROWTH FROM LEAD

While Monyash's existence was due to water, its prosperity was down to the veins of lead in the limestone around the village. During the mid 14th century the nature and size of the village changed significantly as Monyash prospered with the income from the markets and fairs and also with the growth of the lead mining industry.[136] Although lead mining doesn't appear to have made any individual mine owner rich, it did provide a living for many people and a secondary income for hard-pressed farmers.

At this time many of the inhabitants of Monyash will have been involved both in farming and in stone quarrying and/or lead mining. There were several small stone quarries around the village for both housing stone and the higher value marble and also a large number of small veins of lead providing the chance for villagers to dig for lead to supplement their income, or in some cases, as their main source of income (see Figure 28 and Chapter 15: Monyash Mines and Quarries).

Lead mining soon became big business with a large number of individuals digging and opening up small mines and some larger industrial-scale mines. Between 1460 and 1630 the output of all the lead mines in Derbyshire was around 3,800 loads of ore (about 400 tons) and the county was one of the major national lead producing areas (see Box 14: Lead Mining in Monyash).

Barmote (or Barmoot) courts, responsible for regulating the lead mining industry, had been created in 1288 as King Edward I tried to recover royal lands and rights, in particular those lost during the reign of his father, Henry III. Courts in this area were established in Monyash and Wirksworth. Monyash was the regulatory and administrative centre for lead mining in the High Peak area until the turn of the 19th century. (Wirksworth was the centre for the Low Peak). The Monyash Barmote court was held twice a year at The Bull's Head, on the first Tuesday in April and the first Tuesday in October.[137] In 1814, the Monyash court moved to Wirksworth and, since 1994, the two courts have met together on the 3rd Wednesday in April.[138]

The courts comprised 24 (later reduced to 12 in 1852) miners and people connected with mining. The courts were overseen by a Barmaster who was originally chosen by the members of the court but later became an appointee of the Crown. Part of their remit was settling the many disputes associated with lead mining, such as non payment of wages, and disputes between miners and between miners and the mineral owner. They also allocated rights to mine lead (the ownership of the lead remained with the Crown but was leased to the Duke of Devonshire).

In order to claim mining rights all a man had to do was to demonstrate that he had found a significant amount of ore. He was then allowed to open a mine and claim the ore, subject to giving a dish of ore to the Barmaster. Indeed so important was lead mining to the economy that mining took precedence over land ownership; farmers and landowners were not allowed to interfere with the mine's operations. Not surprisingly there were many disputes between landowners and miners to be settled by the courts.

As the villagers prospered so too did the Church as well as the Duke of Devonshire and other landowners. Over the next few years a number of major extensions were made to the Church taking it up to its present size. In 1348 the Lady Chapel (south transept) was added. Around 1350 the nave was rebuilt, the north and south aisles constructed with 'lean-to' roofs, a north transept and south porch added along with the third section to the tower, along with a small spire (see Box 13: Monyash Church 1100-1600).

One devastating event in the 14th century was the Black Death. Black Death was one of the deadliest pandemics in history and is thought to have been a form of bubonic plague. During 1348 and 1349 this disease wiped out about a third of the population of the country. There were further outbreaks later in the century and a major return in 1603. However, it is not believed to have greatly afflicted Monyash, possibly because of its relatively remote position, though William de Lynford Jr, Lord of the Manor of Monyash, died in 1349, possibly from the Black Death.

Box 14: Lead Mining in Monyash

Lead is a pliable but poisonous metal which was laid down as galena (lead sulphide) into the fissures (gaps) in the limestone around 300 million years ago (see Box 1: The Shaping of the White Peak). Lead has been in common use for thousands of years. In Roman times lead was used extensively for water pipes, water tanks, writing tablets, and also to secure the iron pins used to hold large blocks of limestone together, for example.

By the 17th century lead had become an important commodity; essential for roofs, pipes, water storage, ammunition and lead glazing bars for windows and also as a constituent of pewter used in plates, jugs and goblets.[139] Trading in lead, for domestic use as well as for export, was a major business in England and a vital part of the Derbyshire economy. Around 1643, thousands of people in the county relied upon lead mining and trading for their livelihoods.[140]

It is likely that lead has been mined in and around Monyash since at least Roman times. Lead mining was hard work and dangers were many, such as injury, poisoning from lead dust, underground floods, falling rocks and poisonous and flammable gases such as hydrogen sulphide. However for poor families it was an important chance to make some money. Mining was often carried out on a small scale by individuals to supplement their income from farming.

Mining Law split the lead veins into *meers* around 25-30 metres long. The larger meers were called rakes and could be one or two metres wide. (The word *rake* derives from the Anglo-Saxon meaning narrow path and was adopted by the lead miners.[141]) Once a person made a claim on a meer they had to keep working it otherwise it could be claimed by others. This tended to keep lead mining as a large number of small-scale operations. However there were a small number of large-scale operations which often involved deep mining which had many difficulties, in particular the need to pump large quantities of water out of the mine.

The 1951 Ordnance Survey map shows hundreds of old lead mines around Monyash. There were also a few industrial-scale mines; the remains of some of these are still visible today, in particular Mandale Mine and Magpie Mine (see Chapter 15).

15. MONYASH MINES AND QUARRIES

One of the county's oldest lead mines is Mandale Mine in Lathkill Dale (see Figure 30). We know lead was being mined here in 1288 (see also Box 14: Lead Mining in Monyash).[142] Indeed it is possible that this was the lead mine referred to in the Domesday Book (see Box 11: Monyash and the Domesday Book).

This mine was more recently worked on an industrial scale and capital was invested heavily, by a series of companies, in pumping machinery and the construction of soughs (the tunnels or small canals that took the water from the mines to the nearest river). Just two miles from the village, Lathkill Dale would have looked very different hundreds of years ago. Rather than a tranquil paradise for walkers, it was a busy industrial area with mining equipment scattered around and the air filled with noise and dust. There would have been scores of miners, dozens of carts and ponies moving waste, creating hundreds of spoil heaps (hillocks), and other teams of ponies (called jaggers) taking the lead ore out of the valley from the dozens of mine shafts. Most,

Figure 30 Remains of Mandale Mine's pumping house

Figure 31 Digitally reconstructed pillars and aqueduct at Mandale Mine

but not necessarily all, of them are now covered with concrete slabs, making it not the safest place to wander off the path or let a dog off the lead.

Today walkers down Lathkill Dale may notice four small stone pillars (ranging from around one to four metres high) by the path close to Over Haddon. These are the remains of the six large pillars (originally around 10 metres high) that carried an aqueduct high over the path to drive a large 10.6 metre water wheel that was used to power a pump to remove water from Mandale Mine, 27 metres below the level of the river. Figure 31 is a digitally enhanced picture showing what it would have looked like when the pillars were at their full height with the water trough on top. The leat (canal) begins at a header pond by a weir just below Carter's Mill over half a mile up river from the mine, then it runs along the side of the hill (above the line of the river on the opposite side to the path) towards the aqueduct.

Figure 32 Overgrown water wheel pit for the Lathkill Dale vein

Up the hillside from the pillars can be found the site of the old water wheel and the remains of the engine house that housed the huge, three-valve Cornish steam engine which replaced the water-driven pump (see Figure 30). Mandale Mine (and the Mandale vein of lead), at one time operated by the London Lead Company, was very profitable at times with one big strike in 1820 netting a profit of over £1,000 in six months (at the time miners might only be paid around 10 shillings a week - 50p). However, this mine, like all the others, required continual costly investment not only to dig and wall the mine shafts and build the soughs, but also to pump ever increasing amounts of water from the mines as they reached even greater depths. Mining operations between 1808 and 1836 operated at a loss of over £2,000.[143]

Later that century lead mining appears to have undergone a revival in fortunes with many mines being operated; indeed the village reached its population peak in 1851 (see Chapter 25). The engine house and boiler house for the Cornish steam engine were constructed in 1847. However, in 1852, following a few good years of lead extraction, the high operating cost and the cost of repaying the large investment forced the company to cease operations. Mining continued on a small scale by independent miners.[144]

Four hundred yards further up Lathkill Dale, towards Monyash, ramblers may visit the crumbling house across a small footbridge over the river. This was the home of Thomas Bateman who purchased the Lathkill Dale Mine and the rights to mine the lead in the Lathkill Dale vein in 1825. The house, built in 1830, sits right on top of one of the two stone-lined shafts into the lead mine. (One shaft is accessible down a flight of metal steps.) In one large hollow, a few hundred yards upstream of Bateman's House, are the collapsed remains of the water wheel pit which contained an enormous 16 metre diameter wheel that pumped water out of other shafts, thus allowing mining of the Lathkill Dale vein. Figure 32 shows the remains of the housing for the wheel and just across the river can be seen the remains of the upright that supported the trough carrying water from the leat to power the wheel. Little money was ever made from this vein and by 1861 the house had been deserted.[145] The Lathkill Dale and Mandale Mines together produced less than 3,700 tons of concentrated lead ore between 1750 and 1850.

Ricklow Quarry, closer to Monyash towards the head of the Dale, where spoil heaps of large stones cascade down onto the path, was a stone quarry. This was a substantial operation in 1857.[146] The stone was used for building as well as for marble (polished limestone) (see Box 24: Monyash Marble). A little

Figure 33 Carter's Mill 1826
Reproduced from Lost Buildings of
the Peak District by Lindsey Porter.[153]
Copyright, and reproduced with the kind
permission, of Lindsey Porter.

earlier a Monyash miner, Isaac Beresford (or Isaak Berresford), attempted to mine for lead here and meet up with the vein that runs under Magpie Mine. Recent geological surveys reveal that he was a long way from it. However, there is a small lead vein here. He was jailed for debt in 1828.

Hardrake Quarry, known locally as Once-a-Week Quarry (near Sheldon), is the only quarry still operating around Monyash and is now owned by the Mandale Stone Co Ltd at Rowsley. The limestone here is light grey and finely grained with plenty of fossils. It is suggested that its name came from the fact that the miners here were paid weekly, unlike other quarries which paid their men monthly. Alternatively it was an apt description of the level of activity at the quarry.

There were other smaller limestone/marble quarries, including Brecks (or Bricks) Quarry which was located between Monyash and Flagg and is visible off Monyash Dale Road. There were also three corn mills in Lathkill Dale (one of which may have been mentioned in the Domesday Survey). The nearest to Monyash was at Carter's Mill, named after Joseph Carter of Over Haddon.[147] Figure 33 shows a picture of the mill before it was demolished. A mill stone is still visible by the side of the path close to the site of the old mill.

Three other major lead mines lie on the Flagg/Sheldon side of the village. Records about Hubberdale (Hubbadale) Mine in Flagg go back to the 1660s. This mine covered a large area between the Jarnett and Flagg Lane (see Figure 28) and had several shafts, including the Fidler shaft which is thought to be 70 metres deep and floods to a height of 66 metres in winter. It is thought its sough goes into Deepdale. There are many lead veins in this area and in 1776 the miners struck a particularly good one and the mine made a profit of over £21,000 in the following three years.[148] The Greensward (Greensa) Mine, mentioned as far back as the late 16th century, includes a long rake which follows the boundary between Monyash and Ashford, which led to many disputes (see Chapter 13). The rake crosses Horse Lane at the brow of the hill, by the Monyash Parish boundary stone on the left hand side, 200 metres before Barker Fields Farm. It then goes south east towards the Bakewell to Monyash Road, and north east towards Dyke Head Farm, with at least four shafts along its length (see Figure 28). At the end of the 18th century it was owned by William Bonsall who lived at Manor House (then called Rake End Farm) and was not profitable.[149] In the 1860s it was owned by John and George Goodwin also of Monyash.[150]

While there is little above-ground evidence of the Hubberdale and Greensward mines, the remains of another mine, Magpie Mine, can be seen and visited on the outskirts of the village towards Sheldon (see Figure 34). This mine was worked from around 1740. In the 1760s it was owned by George Goodwin of Monyash. Mr Goodwin made little from the mine and, after passing through several other owners, it made a reasonable profit for a few years around 1820. The five million gallons of water which flowed from the sough every day demonstrated the size of the problem the mine owners faced. In 1879 while extending the sough the miners managed to cut off the spring water supply to Sheldon village, creating an additional problem for the mine's owners. Over the next 70 years the problems were compounded by several legal disputes and some very hard rock (toadstone – the miners' name for the very hard layers of igneous rocks). Furthermore, with falling lead prices, the availability of cheaper imports and the progressive removal of an import duty on imported lead[151] coupled with declining demand due to the use of iron and later copper pipes, the lead mine closed in 1883. However, an attempt to rescue the mine was made in 1953 when diesel engines were used to pump water out from a depth of 188 metres. Magpie Mine, the last operating lead mine in the area, was worked intermittently until 1958. Still visible on the Magpie Mine site is the agent's cottage, the smithy, the winding house and boiler house, the square chimney, built in 1840, and the round chimney, built by Cornish workers who introduced new methods of mining around 1869. The shaft by the Cornish Engine house reached 200 metres. The site is now a preserved museum and is operated by the Peak District Mines Historical Society. A public footpath runs through the site and organised parties can be arranged to visit the buildings.[152]

Besides the legacy of mine workings and the hillocks visible around the village, mining has also left a legacy of names, such as Pansy Hillocks near Cross Lanes, Rakes Road and Bole Hill, which was a smelting site in a remote location away from the village due to the poisonous nature of the fumes given off.

Figure 34 Remains of Magpie Mine

16. PUBLIC HOUSES

Farming, stone quarry working and lead mining were all very physically demanding jobs. It was evident that these workers enjoyed quenching their thirst as in 1579 the parish of Monyash had five public houses (pubs). The pubs were The Bull's Head, The Bull i' th' Thorn, The Golden Lion, The Star and The Bay Horse. In 1589 five villagers, presumably the landlords of the five pubs, were taken to the High Peak court sitting in Chapel-en-le-Frith for selling short measures. Roger Redfern, Alice Needham, Hugh Rogers, Bryan Ireland and Alice Swindell were each fined 2d (two old pence).[154]

These were not like today's pubs. They were simple 'ale shops' with a few chairs and tables in a front room. The 'landlord' would brew ales and stouts in an outhouse though their prime income may have come from other sources such as farming. Making and selling beer was a means of supplementing their income and taking some of the benefits from the lead mining.

The Bull's Head is still operating by the village green (see Figures 1 and 35). It is likely that there has been a building here for hundreds of years, if not a thousand or so years. The building, which was a farm a few hundred years ago, has been rebuilt several times. The oldest part of the current building has a lintel above the old doorway dated 1619 with the initials HG and EG. These are thought to refer to Humphrey and Elizabeth Goodwin who were freeholders of Monyash in 1633 (see Figure 36).[155] From the 14th century onwards it would have provided lodging for visitors, such as merchants, and stabling for their horses.

The Bull i' th' Thorn, at the edge of the parish on the A515, also dates back hundreds of years. The beam above the fireplace is dated 1472 with other carvings on the panelling dated to 1642 and 1742. The Bull i' th' Thorn sits alongside the old Roman road (the earlier Neolithic trackway). It is at a slight angle to the current road showing that the old road originally ran parallel to the front of the pub then across the fields to Endmoor and then Arbor Low. Originally a farm it would have been a Roman staging post along the Roman road. It is thought to have originally been called The Bull later being renamed Hurdlow Thorn, changing its name to Hurdlow House in 1654, then at some point to its current name. During the 18th and 19th centuries it was a coaching inn on the Derby to Manchester turnpike (see Chapter 24).[156]

Figure 35 The Bull's Head, smithy and market cross circa 1920

The Golden Lion was on Church Street and was the most recent pub to close in the village (see Figure 37). The pub was called the Golden Fleece in 1857.[157] During the late 19th and early 20th centuries the pub was the meeting place for the Monyash Friendly Society (see Chapter 29). The Society met there until the pub closed around 1919, moving its meetings to The Bull's Head. The pub is now two private houses; Lathkill House and Lathkill Cottage.

Melbourne House on Chapel Street used to be The Star public house. It is believed to have been rebuilt in 1704 and at some point also had tea rooms. The Bay Horse Inn, now called the Old Bay Horse Inn, was on Chapel Street. This was possibly the smallest of the village pubs. There is a vaulted cellar below the house which was used to keep the beer cool. At one time one of the mine owners lived next door in Sheldon House, where the workers would be paid weekly. It was just a small stride from there to The Bay Horse.

**Figure 36 The Bull's Head
1619 date stone**

Figure 37 The Golden Lion 1910
Walter Lomas, the proprietor, with his children outside The Golden Lion

17. MONYASH ON THE MAP

As the village developed so did its network of tracks and roads. The roads were important to bring in traders to the markets and also take out the lead and stone on packhorses. They were also important for 'through traffic'. The saltway that passed close to the village, across Derby Lane, carried salt from the mines of Cheshire to Bakewell, Chesterfield and beyond. The wide green lanes around the village were used by drovers moving sheep or cattle from farm to market. (See Box 15: Packhorse Ways, Saltways and Drovers' Roads).

Finding your way across the moorland areas was not easy and instructions were passed verbally from person to person. There were no maps or signposts or guide stones to help the traveller. It would also appear that many of the tracks around the country were in poor condition so an Act of Parliament in 1555 made each parish responsible for the upkeep of the highways and ordered that each householder had to work four days a year (upped to six days in 1563) on maintaining the parish highways.[158]

As the packhorse was slowly replaced by various horse-drawn wheeled vehicles, the tracks gradually improved eventually resulting in the creation of turnpikes (well constructed roads) in the 17th century – see Chapter 24. It is said that the first coach to be seen in the Peak was the one carrying Mary Queen of Scots around 1570.[159]

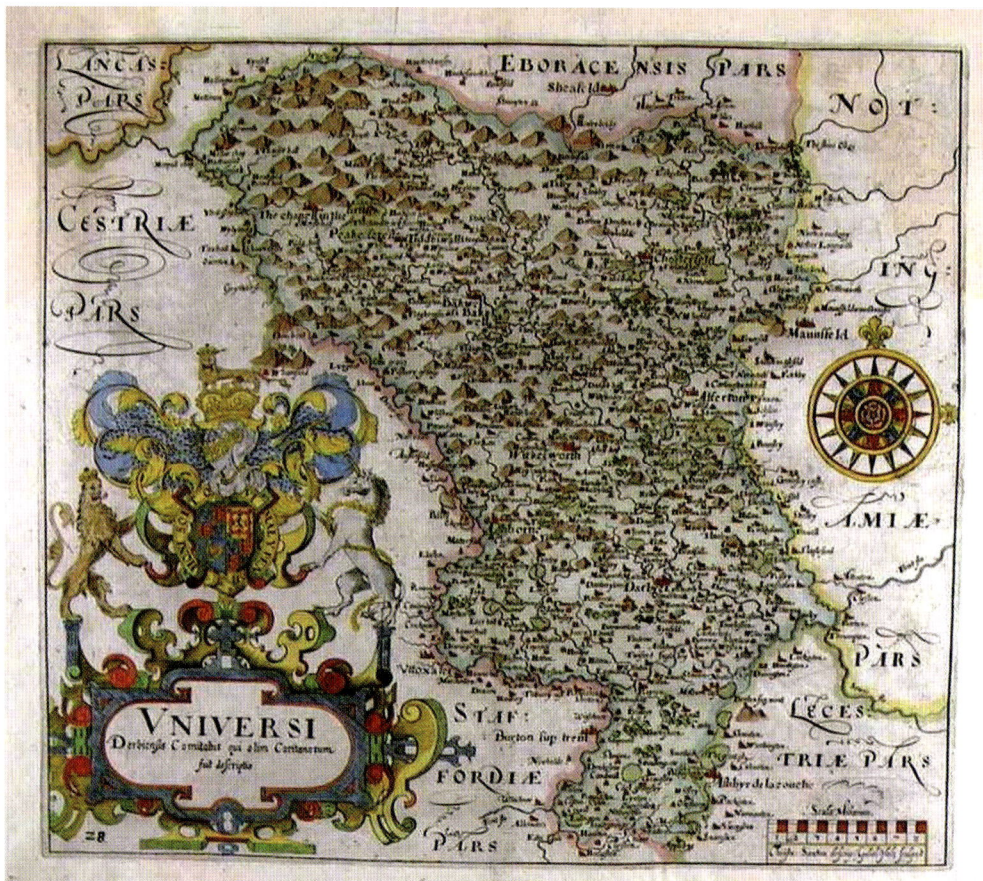

Figure 38 Saxton, Hole and Kip's map of Derbyshire 1637

Figure 39 The four sides of the guide stone on Derby Lane

Monyash first appeared on a map when the first map of Derbyshire was produced in 1577 by Christopher Saxton. Saxton, (c1543 - c1610) a Yorkshire man, was commissioned to survey the whole of England and Wales. This took him around seven years to complete. However his maps did not show the tracks but just the main topographical features. The map (Figure 38) shows Derbyshire, including Monyash, on a later version by Saxton which was engraved by William Hole and William Kip and published in 1637.

Such maps were of little use to travellers who often had difficulty finding their way over the rough and open terrain, especially in poor weather. An Act of Parliament in 1697 not only tried to improve the condition of roads and encourage the building of stone packhorse bridges, but also instructed that guide posts (usually wooden finger posts) should be erected in remote areas showing the way to the nearest towns.[160] However, it was not until after a law passed in 1709 that guide posts were erected in Derbyshire, following the threat of legal action by the Government. Stone guide posts were favoured in North Derbyshire (sometimes called guide stoops – stoop from the Old Norse for stone). One such guide stone can still be found, in its original location, on Derby Lane (the 'alternative' route from Derby to Manchester via Monyash, Flagg and Chelmorton). The stone is at the crossing point between Derby Lane and the saltway from Cheshire to Bakewell (GR 157651). This large limestone post (now a gatepost) has four faces which read Bvxton, Chedel, Darby and Bakewel (see Figure 39). On the Buxton side are also the letters BR, the initials of the surveyor (reporting to the courts) who inspected it.[161]

In 1675 the Derby to Buxton route still followed the Roman road close to Grangemill, through Pikehall, then close to Arbor Low, with Monyash off to the east, joining up with the present A515 by The Bull i' th' Thorn until the Duke of York. Robert Morden's map of 1701 shows the main road from Derby to Manchester taking the line of the Roman road past Monyash (in the High Peak Hundred). A later map by John Carey in 1783 (see Figure 40) shows the main road through Monyash as the current road from Longnor, via Endmoor down Tagg Lane then to Ashford. This also shows the track, via Cross Lane, direct to Flagg and the existing road going off to Taddington, with also a minor road to Bakewell. The Roman road is still shown as a track/road to Pikehall.

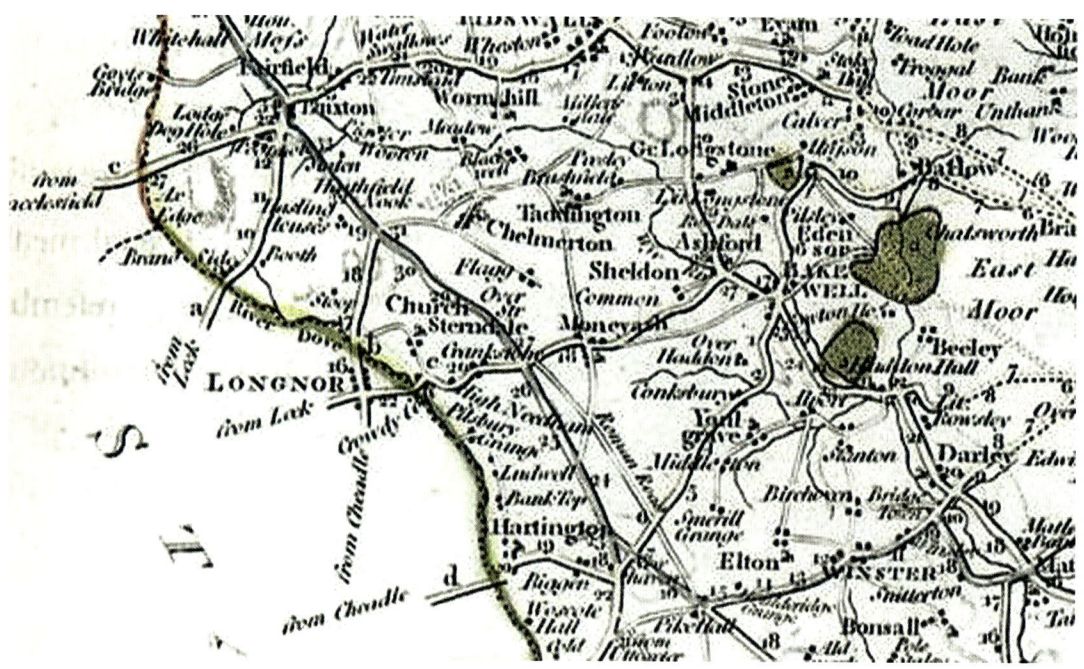

Figure 40 Section of Carey's map of 1783 with Moneyash in the centre

Box 15: Packhorse Ways, Saltways and Drovers' Roads

Packhorse ways were developed to allow packhorses, with their load in two panniers or baskets on either side of the saddle, to travel over the rough ground and the moors between the towns and villages (unlike the Roman roads which were primarily used for getting armies and supplies quickly from one fort to the next). Teams of packhorses, and later horses and carts, could cover long distances with their loads. Their cargos might include lead ore or marble (see Box 24: Monyash Marble) from the local mines, copper from Ecton (mined since the Bronze Age), food stuffs, clothes, grains and chert from the mine at Holme Bank in Bakewell used in the Potteries for grinding a whitening agent, pots from Staffordshire and stoneware pottery from Chesterfield. Many packhorse bridges still survive in the area, such as at Conksbury over the Lathkill, near Over Haddon, together with Packhorse Inns at Crowdicote and Little Longstone. Occasionally the horses and their drivers were hit by bad weather and it has been known for them to starve and/or freeze to death. Apparently John Allcock, a blacksmith, and Richard Boham, a baker, died on Middleton Common (just east of Arbor Low) in a snowstorm when they were returning to Hartington from Winster Market in 1772. They went missing on the night of Saturday 31st January and their bodies were not found until the Monday.[162]

Another common load was salt, used to preserve meat, and so some packhorse ways became known as saltways. Salt was moved from the Cheshire area on routes through the Peak District, such as via Denton and then on to North and West Yorkshire, and to Sheffield via Chapel-en-le-Frith, or to Chesterfield via Buxton. One saltway passed through Monyash en route for Bakewell then Chesterfield and beyond. This track did not go through the middle of the village but crossed over Derby Lane a mile or so outside of the village at the site of the old guide stone (see Chapter 17). This route from Cheshire went via Pilsbury then close to Custard Field, crossing the A515 at the bend in the road just north of Moscar Farm. It then followed what is now a footpath crossing the old Roman road north of the tumulus at Benty Grange, then along what is now a wide green lane, crossing the Parsley Hay to Monyash road at GR 149646. The saltway then went across what was once open common land (later enclosed, see Box 21: The Monyash Enclosure Act 1771) direct to the guide stone (GR 157651), then down Fern (also called Fere or Fear) Dale (recently opened as a concessionary footpath) to the top of Lathkill Dale and up the other side of the Dale on to Over Haddon via the unnamed minor road that goes past Haddon Grove Farms (and camp site) to Over Haddon then Bakewell possibly via Intake Lane.

All these tracks were also used by drovers. These people (the haulage contractors of their day) moved cattle or sheep either from one grazing area to another or from farm to market, often covering long distances. The herds could be large with a couple of hundred cattle or a thousand sheep being moved at a time by several drovers. The animals for market were only taken short distances each day as the best prices came from animals in the best condition. Frequent watering stops were needed and Monyash was a prime location with its five meres providing a reliable supply of water and several inns for food and lodging.[163]

18. THE CHURCH FALLS INTO DISREPAIR 1600-1800

Despite a doubling of the population of Monyash, from around 200 to around 400, between 1600 and 1880 (see Chapter 25) various parts of the Church building fell into disrepair. At some time between 1550 and 1650 the north transept was in poor condition and eventually collapsed. Rather than rebuild the north transept it was walled up. During this period parts of the south porch also fell down and were not repaired.

There are several possible reasons for this lack of investment. First, the support and patronage of a single lord of the manor was lost as the manor of Monyash was broken up on the death of Lord Gilbert the 7th Earl of Shrewsbury in 1616 (see Box 12: Lords of the Manor of Monyash 1066-1721). Second, the Church lost some local support as some of the parishioners became Quakers towards the end of the 17th century, or Methodists in the early 19th century. And third, to make matters worse, many of the lead mine owners who became Quakers refused to pay the taxes due to the Church (see Box 16: Monyash Quakers and Box 17: Methodists and Monyash).

Figure 41 St Leonard's Church pre-1886

Monyash Church received a boost in 1650 following a review by parliamentary commissioners, when it was made independent of Bakewell and became a parish church in its own right. Ralph Roades was the minister at the time.

Later in 1742, during the reign of King George II, the Royal Coat of Arms was constructed, painted and hung, as was common practice, to recognise the sovereign as head of the Church. Royal Arms were usually hung above the chancel arch but in Monyash it is on the west wall of the nave above the tower arch.[164] (This Royal Arms is now one of the few remaining Royal Arms in Derbyshire. It was renovated in 2010 at a cost of £2,400.)

In 1827 the Rev R R Rawlins visited Monyash as part of his tour of Derbyshire churches and chapels.[165] He reported that there was no sign of the north transept and a drawing he made shows buttresses in place where the transept walls used to be. He also confirmed that the south porch was dilapidated. In his report he described a church with a tower and spire. The nave and aisles had double-pitched (▲ shaped) roofs quite different to the mono-pitch (◣ shaped, or lean-to) that we see today on the aisles. The south transept's roof extended out from the south aisle's roof, again double-pitched. Today it is also double-pitched but the roof line is at 90 degrees to the previous one. A photograph dating back to the mid to late 19th century (Figure 41) clearly shows the double-pitched roofs and confirms that the nave and chancel roofs were lower than they are today (Figure 42). The remains of the roof line on the tower wall shows the height of the roof before it was lowered toward the end of the 15th century (see Box 13: Monyash Church 1100-1600). Rawlins also reported that the internal ceilings were all flat and plastered and part of the ceiling to the chancel hid a considerable portion of the chancel arch.

Figure 42 St Leonard's Church 2010

19. CHARITIES TO SUPPORT THE POOR OF MONYASH

Just as the Church was in need of funds some of the villagers of Monyash were living in great poverty. Several charities were set up around this time for the benefit of the local poor, widows and fatherless children. The earliest, a bequest by Ralph Rider on his death in 1709, provided money to the poor of both Monyash and Little Longstone from rent from land in Monyash. This charity is still in existence today. Other charities were also created by benefactors such as John Bartholomew in 1720 and George Goodwin in 1724. Both are now within a trust administered by the Church of England. A later one set up in 1818 by the Rev Francis Gisborne, who was rector of Staveley Church, still supports several parishes today. The Rev Gisborne placed over £13,000 in trust, a very substantial sum at the time, "for providing flannel and coarse woollen cloth for the poor of the several rectories, vicarages, curacies and chapel-ries, being 100 in number".[166] The money was invested and the interest paid annually to the vicars of around 100 parishes, including Monyash, for distribution to the deserving. Francis Gisborne died in July 1821 and, after other bequests, he had instructed that his property was divided up between Sheffield and Derby Infirmaries (hospitals) with the remaining third added into his charity.[167]

In November 1823 Thomasin Palfreyman, of Crag Hall, Cheshire, bequeathed £100 to be invested in land, the rent from which was to be given in clothing to the poor of Monyash and the neighbourhood on Christmas Eve. The land purchased was Soldier's Croft. She also put aside an additional sum of £5.5s.0d. (£5.25) to erect a tablet in the Church near the south door mentioning the bequest.[168] Thomasin, who died in 1837, is buried in the churchyard at Monyash.

In 1825 Hugh Goodwin also provided a trust, the interest from which, around £10 a year, was to be distributed to poor of the village. He also paid to expand the land available to support the School.

20. QUAKERS IN MONYASH

While some parishioners needed the support of charity, the Church was also struggling for investment and, to make its situation worse, there was a new religious force in Monyash which refused to provide money for, and the taxes due to, the Church. In the 17th century Monyash became a centre for Derbyshire Quakers and they invested heavily in the mines, owning many of them and recruiting the workforce from their fraternity.[169] John Gratton, one of their most famous and influential brothers, lived in Monyash for 34 years (see Box 16: Monyash Quakers). On his death he left his cottage and some land, the cottage becoming the Friends' Meeting House, the Quaker Chapel (see

Figure 43 The Quaker Chapel 2010

Figure 43). The graveyard behind the chapel contains the remains of many local Quakers including many of the Bowman family (see Figure 44). This building is currently unused. However, the Quakers reserve the right to make use of the building. It is believed that planning permission was granted some years ago for the Chapel to be converted into a Quaker hostel.

Figure 44 Quaker graveyard with some of the Bowman graves

Box 16: Monyash Quakers

The Religious Society of Friends, whose members are known as Quakers or Friends, was founded in the 17th century by people who were dissatisfied with the existing Christian sects and their forms of worship. George Fox, an apprentice shoemaker from Leicestershire, was one of the principal co-founders. At 19 he experienced a divine call and became an itinerant evangelist during which time he realised that the voice of Christ came from within.[170] Quakers share a way of life rather than a set of beliefs and seek to experience God directly, within themselves and in their relationships with others and the world around them, meeting together for silent worship. Their focus is on their experiences rather than written statements of belief.[171] This approach brought Fox and the Quakers into conflict with the established Church as they refused to acknowledge the status of ministers or pay tithes to the Church. Indeed Fox derisorily referred to churches as steeplehouses.

John Gratton who lived in Monyash for 34 years was one of the early converts. He was born in Bakewell in 1641 and died in 1711. Although a Presbyterian, in 1664 he found himself questioning the Church's style of ministry. He moved to Monyash in 1668 where he lived until 1702. In 1671, a few years after meeting a Quaker woman in 1664, while riding on the road to Sheldon, he realised that the Quakers were his people. He then became a Quaker and began preaching all over the country. Despite initial scepticism and mockery by the local people, John Gratton recruited many followers in Monyash and established a group of Quakers in the village.[172] In 1689 there were 12 Quakers living in Monyash including Gratton and his wife.

A little earlier, in 1682, William Penn, a Quaker, founded the state of Pennsylvania and many Quaker families emigrated there, including Richard Nailer from Monyash.[173]

Although the Quakers have a history of notable commercial successes based on strong Christian principles inseparable from their acts of philanthropy, they did not have an easy time. They had goods confiscated and were subjected to local rough justice and even imprisonment for crimes such as blasphemy and refusing to contribute to the parish church. Despite the 1662 Quakers Act which prohibited their assembly for worship, Gratton preached for many years in the area including Darley Dale, Matlock, Alfreton, Brampton, Tideswell, Chesterfield, Nottingham and Mansfield. Although he was frequently arrested he usually managed to escape jail and was let off with a £20 fine thanks to a sympathetic Earl of Devonshire, who was then Lord-Lieutenant, and the local justice, Sir Henry Every.[174] However, Gratton had some enemies, most notably Thomas Wilson, a newly appointed vicar of Bakewell. In August 1680 Gratton was arrested in Bakewell and imprisoned in Derby jail for six years. While there he helped his jailer by getting his son a job in London with a goldsmith. As a result the jailer allowed him the run of his house and garden and he was even allowed out of prison to address various meetings. On one occasion he managed to attend a funeral in Monyash; seeing government agents he raced back to the Derby jail to confound the investigators who came to check on him, much to the relief of his jailer.[175]

Gratton was apparently a very hospitable man. According to one of the many testimonials contained at the start of Gratton's book about his life, thirteen Friends wrote, "Whilst he lived in Monyash, in the county of Derby, his house and heart were open, his entertainment's free: the company of honest Friends was very acceptable and many made respectful visits to him, which he would say were times of comfort and consolation".[176]

On his death on 9th January 1711 at the age of 69, he left a cottage and some ground in Monyash to the Society of Friends. The cottage was converted into a Friends' Meeting House (the Quaker Chapel).[177] The building was completed in 1717 six years after his death. The Meeting House has a small graveyard containing several simple gravestones, mainly of the Bowmans of One Ash Grange.

On his death some of his Friends in Monyash wrote the following testimonial:

"We whose names are subscribed below, being members of Monyash monthly meeting, to which our well beloved friend, John Gratton, did many years belong, in which time we were intimately acquainted with him; enjoyed many comfortable and precious opportunities in conversing together, and were often refreshed under his ministry. We find ourselves concerned, as a duty we owe to his memory, and for the recommending his Christian labours to succeeding ages, to write this brief testimony concerning him. He was a man of note in his country, and one whose Christianity did show itself in the spirit of meekness and humility, notwithstanding many troubles and exercises which he met with. He was also an able minister of the everlasting gospel, being made instrumental in the convincement of many. He had great openings, was sound in doctrine, and skilful in hitting the mark. His ministry was lively and powerful, plentifully opening the Scriptures. He travelled much in the service of Truth, both in this nation, and in other countries adjacent. His residence was at Monyash, in the county of Derby, above forty years, where we were often comforted in his company, and therefore loved him in the Truth, and do believe that he lived and died a servant of the Lord. He departed this life at Farnsfield, in Nottinghamshire, in the sixty-ninth year of his age.

[signed by]
Elihu Hall
Rebecca Bowman
Henry Bowman
Ann Bowman
Cornelius Bowman
Sarah Potter
George Potter
Hester Bowman."[178]

21. MONYASH METHODISTS

As the evangelical fervour of the Quakers began to decline in the middle of the 18th century, Christian evangelism was taken up by a second breakaway religious movement, Methodism (see Box 17: Methodists and Monyash). The Methodist movement began in the late 1720s and soon spread across the country as a result of John Wesley's preaching. At the time there were few chapel buildings as the Methodists were 'open air' evangelical preachers, or worshipped in private houses, which added to "their domestic and friendly appeal".[179]

Methodism was not universally welcomed into Monyash and there were reports of a disturbance in 1742 when the Rev John Bennett, a close friend of John Wesley and a popular and powerful preacher,[180] was preaching in the village. (Other sources suggest the preacher was John Nelson, a stonemason.[181]) The then priest at St Leonard's, the Rev Robert Lomas, accompanied by a band of lead miners, somewhat worse for drink, tried to drown out the singing and to overturn the chairs the preacher was using during prayers, even tearing at the preacher's clothes. Bennett described the scene.

"When I went into the Peak to preach at Monyash when a clergyman with a great company of men that worked in the lead mines, all being in liquor, came in just as I was about to give out the hymn. As soon as we began to sing he began to halloo and shout as if he were hunting with a pack of hounds, and so continued all the time we sang. When I began to pray, he attempted to overturn the chair I stood on, but he could not, although he struck it so violently with his feet that he broke one of the arms of the chair right off. When I began to preach he called on one of his companions to pull me down, but he replied, 'No, Sir, the man says nothing but the truth; pray hold your peace and let us hear what he has to say.'"

The Rev Lomas then examined Bennett's Bible and said "It is a right Bible, and if you preach by the spirit of God, then let me hear you from this Text, which has wisdom to strengthen the wise, more than ten mighty men in a city…." The parson agreed and after a while the report suggests that many were in tears and they left to allow the preacher to continue in peace.[182]

Reputedly one villager was so upset by the actions of the Reverend that he forecast the vicar would die a dreadful death. Indeed the Rev Lomas did meet an untimely and unpleasant end (see Box 20: The Legend of Parson's Tor).

The tensions between the Methodists and Anglicans continued for many years. Miss Smales, the Monyash school teacher (who retired in 1924), was not initially allowed to teach because it was discovered that her father was a Methodist preacher.

As the Methodist movement grew it invested in the building of chapels and schools. By 1825 there were more than 15,000 Methodist supporters in Derbyshire and many chapels for worship.[183] In 1835 the original Monyash Primitive Methodist Chapel was constructed. This is now the 'school room', and the later, larger extension, built in 1888, is now the main Chapel (see Figures 8 and 45 and Box 17: Methodists and Monyash).

Box 17: Methodists and Monyash

Three evangelical missionaries, John Wesley (who was a Church of England clergyman), his brother Charles and George Whitefield, began what would become known as the Methodist movement in the late 1720s. After a spell in America, on 1st May 1739 John Wesley and his followers formed the first Methodist Society in London. In the same year they built the first chapel in Bristol. However they were predominantly 'open air preachers' and established Methodist societies as they travelled the country. Wesley is reputed to have preached over 40,000 sermons and travelled a quarter of a million miles claiming "I look upon the whole world as my parish". Wesley never came to Monyash but got close; he twice went to Chelmorton.

Other early pioneers of the Methodist (Wesleyan) movement who did preach in Monyash included John Bennett, Richard Boardman and John Nelson, a renowned Yorkshire stonemason and one of the most widely known of John Wesley's lay assistants.

Wesley and his fellow preachers encouraged people to work hard and save for the future. They also had a lot to say about personal morality and the dangers of gambling and drinking. John Wesley was very supportive of female preachers and he also encouraged people who had full-time jobs to become lay preachers. This gave working people valuable experience of speaking in public and involved them in the activities of the Church. After Wesley's death in 1791, the Methodists formally separated from the Anglican Church.

The Bakewell Methodist circuit was set up in 1808 and by 1825 Monyash was a designated preaching location with services held at 10.00, followed by a service at Flagg at 2.00 on alternate Sundays.

Figure 45 Inside the Methodist Chapel

In 1829 a young Monyash quarryman, named Joshua Millington, was converted to Methodism. He later became a local preacher, a task he continued to undertake for over 60 years (see Box 23: Monyash Tradespersons – 1846).

In the 1830s and 40s the Methodists started an ambitious and expensive programme of chapel and school building.[184] The first Chapel in Monyash was built on the site of a house or the house may have been converted into a chapel. The new larger Chapel was added in 1888. There are seven foundation stones round the building which were donated and laid by leading villagers; Charles Critchlow, J Caleb Millington, William Palfreyman, John Hibbert, Richard Dunn, William Critchlow and James D Harrison. The new Chapel cost just over £600 to build including the purchase of the additional land. Villagers provided £35 worth of labour themselves. A storeroom was later added around 1945.

The Chapel also has its own Christmas carols; Awake, Hark and Old Hark. A new electronic organ was installed in 1957 and found to be 'hopeless', so it was replaced shortly afterwards by a fine pipe organ (see Figure 45).

Box 18: The Cheney Family

The Cheney family can be traced back to Ralph de Caineto (also known as Ralph Cheine) who arrived with William the Conqueror. Members of the family had a tradition of serving the King as sheriffs or other officers.[185] They were a large and influential family, some of whom lived in and around Monyash for much of the 18th century.

Sir John Cheney, the 1st Baron Cheney of Shurland, was the great hero of the family. He was born in Shurland, Eastchurch, Kent around 1447, the eldest son of John Cheney and Eleanor Shottesbroke. Sir John was also Lord of the Manor of Beeley, a manor purchased by the family sometime during the 13th century.[186] He fought for King Henry VII during the Wars of the Roses and was ennobled as a Knight Banneret after the Battle of Stoke on 16th June 1487, becoming Lord Cheney of Falstone Cheney. At the Battle of Bosworth Field 22nd August 1485, when Henry Tudor defeated King Richard III ending the Plantagenet dynasty and starting the Tudor reign, Cheney was one of Henry's bodyguards. Legend has it that King Richard charged towards Henry to eliminate his rival, killing William Brandon, Henry's standard bearer, and unhorsing Cheney with a blow to the head. Dazed and bleeding Cheney cut the skull and horns from an ox hide and fixed it on his head to hold the wound together and provide some protection, allowing him to fight on. Richard too continued fighting but was cut down, becoming the last English king to die on the field of battle on English soil. Cheney's feats in the battle so impressed Henry Tudor that when he was crowned Henry VII he assigned Sir John the Bull's Head and scalp as a crest, which his descendants continue to bear. The Bull's Head in Monyash is reputedly named after this event.

Cheney was also made a Knight of the Garter. He joined parliament in 1487 and in 1497 married the widow of Baron Stourton, becoming Lord Stourton (he was 82 and she 53 – it was a marriage to gain lands and prestige). He died in 1499 without children.[187] His estates were inherited by his nephew, Thomas Cheney. Thomas, who was knighted in 1513, was also close to King Henry VII, and at one time Treasurer of his household and a Privy Councillor. On his death in 1558 his son Henry inherited his land, including Ashford Hall in Derbyshire.

Sir Thomas's great-great-great-great grandson, also Thomas Cheney, is believed to have built Hall Croft, the now dilapidated building near the Church in Monyash. (More recently this was the home of John Hibbert, coal merchant, whose name appears on one of the foundation stones in the Methodist Chapel. He had the house built next door, reputedly, being a staunch Methodist, from the money he had not spent on beer and tobacco.) Thomas Cheney also built Manor House (then called Rake End Farm) in 1714 (see Figure 46).[188] It was the largest house in the village at the time.[189] Thomas Cheney died on 30th September 1723 aged 62 years, and there is a memorial to him and his wife, Jane (or Johanna), who died in November 1724 also 62 years old, in the Lady Chapel at St Leonard's Church.

In 1721 Edward Cheney, Thomas's son, purchased some of the land around Monyash from three owners to become the Lord of the Manor of Monyash.[190] Monyash was mainly in the hands of the Cheney family until 1861. Robert Henry Cheney of Shiffnal (Edward's great-great grandson) appears to have had little interest in Monyash while living a high bachelor life style in Shropshire. He sold the manor of Monyash on 17th October 1861 (see Chapter 26: Monyash – The Grand Sale).[191]

Figure 46 Manor Farm right with Ivy Cottage left circa 1910

22. MONYASH SCHOOL

The Primary School was built in 1752 to educate the poor children of Monyash, four years old and upwards. The villagers raised £200 from donations including the sale of five acres of land, part of the Common of Monyash, for £75, to Edward Cheney, Lord of the Manor. This paid for the cost of erecting the School and investments in land, including two small strips of about an acre in total, on the right hand side of Rakes Road leaving the village, to provide a £10 per year salary to the school master (see Box 19: Monyash Primary School). [192]

The School is located in the centre of the village at the crossroads. (This area used to be part of a large open space and was likely the original market square.) The rear of the School used to look over Cow Mere (see Figure 47). This mere was filled in during the 1950s and is now used as the School playing field. The playing field is owned by the Parish Council.

Figure 47 The School and pupils by Cow Mere circa 1910

The building adjacent to the School (the larger building on the left in Figure 47), which used to be the head teacher's house and more recently privately rented, became available in 1989. With some financial assistance from the Integrated Rural Development Scheme (see Chapter 32), the villagers renovated the building and created a much needed second classroom downstairs and staff room and storage space upstairs. The School use the village hall for PE, school lunches and concerts.

Inside the infant play area, behind the School, is a well, which is securely sealed, but a visible reminder of the importance of wells and springs in Monyash's past.

Box 19: Monyash Primary School

On the 4th August 1752 a deed was drawn up between several freeholders (landowners) of Monyash, including George Goodwin, George Barker, George Newton together with the Duke of Devonshire and Edward Cheney, Lord of the Manor of Monyash, to set aside a piece of "waste ground in the centre of the village, containing 30 yards by 20, lying before the ancient pool [Cow Mere]" as the location for the school. [193]

Nine people were appointed as Trustees including William, Duke of Devonshire, Sir Nathanial Curzon, Edward Cheney, George Barker and George Newton, and charged with using the money raised from donations to build the School and also invest enough to provide for £10 a year to pay for a school master. He was to be a "man of sober and discreet carriage and behaviour, of good name and fame and shall be at least versed in the English tongue and master of good plain writing and understands vulgar [basic] arithmetic". He could expect to be sacked through "drunkenness, profaneness or immorality". He was to teach the "Legal poor" children of the village, at no charge, in reading, writing and arithmetic "and in the principles of the Christian Religion of the Church of England". [194]

Following the Monyash Enclosure Act of 1771, the School was also given a field of 14 acres and 32 perches (about six hectares) to increase the income for the School (see Box 21: The Monyash Enclosure Act 1771).

In 1833 the government provided money for the construction of schools, and in 1880 the Elementary Education Act made education compulsory from the ages of five to twelve. As a result of the increase in pupils the School was enlarged in 1890. In 1891 there were 103 children registered at Monyash School though the average attendance was only 70.[195] Pupils were split into two classes run by Mr John Jones Morgan, the headmaster, and Mrs Mary Ann Morgan, the infant class mistress.[196]

Another Act in 1918 raised the school leaving age to 14, leading to the creation of many secondary/high schools, reducing the burden on small village (now primary) schools though in 1922 Monyash School still had around 100 pupils from the age of five to 14. It was not until the Butler Education Act of 1944 that the split between primary and secondary schools at the age of 11 came about.

By 1989, the School had around 45 children with its two classes still taught in one room, separated by a curtain, with little space for anything else. Meals were, and still are, taken in the village hall, which is also used for PE. The School was enlarged when the adjacent house, which years before used to be the school master's house, became vacant. With the help of money from the Integrated Rural Development Scheme (see Chapter 32) the villagers converted this into a second classroom with an office and storage space upstairs. More recently the toilets have been upgraded and a small extension has been constructed for use as a tuition room or office.

The School is now a voluntary controlled school with the buildings and land belonging to the Diocesan Education Authority.

Box 20: The Legend of Parson's Tor

The Rev Robert Lomas was the parish priest from 1732 and was reputed to have been responsible for planting, or overseeing the planting of, the lime trees in the churchyard. He married a local girl, Mary Palfreyman, in Chelmorton Church and they had seven children. There is a record of his son, Exuperius, being baptised in the Monyash Church in 1753.[197]

Rev Lomas met an untimely death in Lathkill Dale on the night of 11th October 1776. He is said to have lost his way whilst returning to Monyash from Bakewell and fell over a precipice between Lathkill and Ricklow Dales. This rock was known as Fox Tor but since then has been known as Parson's Tor. A tuft of grass found clenched in his hand was preserved in a bottle in Monyash up to about 1850.

It is reputed that the wife of a later vicar had, on a number of occasions, seen the figure of a clergyman standing in the Church, and she had always felt 'cheered and comforted' as a result of these appearances. She was quite convinced that it was the ghost of Robert Lomas. There have been more recent but unconfirmed sightings. The Rev Robert Lomas is buried in St Leonard's churchyard underneath a yew tree.

23. WALLS, FIELDS, TITHES AND DEW PONDS

Dry stone walls have been in existence in Monyash since early prehistoric times, primarily to keep cattle out of arable land. By the mid-18th century, before the Enclosure (Inclosure) Acts (see Box 21: The Monyash Enclosure Act 1771), most of the land close to the village had been enclosed by walls[198] creating numerous narrow strip fields (ancient enclosures). Each strip was allocated to a tenant farmer and redistributed each year to ensure that everyone got a share of the good and not-so-good land.[199] The village was also surrounded by rough grassland, called common and waste land, and this was a vital part of the medieval economy, where villagers were able to graze their animals, collect brushwood and dig for turf for fuel (turbary).

Some of the land, farmed and common, was owned by a few local farmers, such as Henry John Gisborne and George Goodwin but it was mainly in the hands of the Cheney's, as Lords of the Manor, and the local landed estates, including the Dukes of Devonshire, the Dukes of Rutland, the Curzons and the Church, the Dean and Chapter of Lichfield. The quarrying rights in and around Monyash were also owned by the Cheneys. These landowners were entitled to rent and/or tithes from the tenant farmers; tithes equivalent to ten per cent of their outputs, such as crops, sheep, wool, eggs, cattle and lead.

In the late 18th century the government was under pressure to deal with thousands of disputes over the use of common land and also to try to bring more acres into production to feed the growing populations in the towns and cities. Each area had its own Enclosure Act which provided for the appointment of commissioners to make an award (The Enclosure Award) dividing the common land around the villages and allocating it to those with rights over it, to clear and improve it for farming.[200] These new fields greatly extended the existing field system around Monyash and were much larger than the ancient strip fields close to the village. Miles of new dry stone walls were erected around these new large fields. A look at a recent map of Monyash (or the aerial photograph in Figure 48) shows a clear distinction between the small fields close to the village which tended to follow topographical lines and the larger surrounding, more rectangular, fields which were planned on a map before being allocated and walled (see Box 21: The Monyash Enclosure Act 1771).

The new fields were allocated to those people who had a right to, or rights over, the common land, usually freeholders (local landowning farmers) rather than the tenants. One field was also allocated to provide an additional income for the School and one to the trustees of charities for the poor. The previous owners would have been recompensed through the allocation of some land and/or payments of tithes or money.

Importantly for the villagers, when the common land was enclosed it was the landowners who benefitted. The smallholders and villagers with no legal rights to the common and waste areas lost access to this land which had been a vital part of their livelihood.

There was also pressure on the landowners (not the tenants) to create larger and more productive fields and so it is also likely that some walls between the strip fields close to the village were also removed. Unfortunately for tenant farmers this meant re-negotiation of their terms as an Enclosure Award annulled the leases on land and property. As the land was assumed to be more productive, landowners felt justified in significantly increasing their rents. Public rights of way were also made official. Though they would have followed ancient routes, they now had to be enclosed by walls, and made either 30 or 40 feet (nine or 12 metres) wide to allow grazing to take place. Such lanes are clearly recognisable around the village today.

The Enclosure Awards made by the commissioners (appointed by the Enclosure Act) defined the acreage and dimensions of each new field and also showed who was responsible for the upkeep of the boundary walls. Figure 27 earlier provided a sketch of the ancient fields close to the village and the common and waste grounds around the village that became enclosed. Figure 49 shows the areas beyond the ancient field system that were enclosed and Box 21: The Monyash Enclosure Act 1771, provides a list of the people who were granted the newly enclosed common land by the Monyash Enclosure Awards.

With the greater restriction on the movement of cattle following the Enclosure Awards, Dew ponds (small man-made ponds with a stone base waterproofed with clay) had to be built to collect rain water (not dew). The 19th century method of lining Dew ponds was invented by Mr Dew, after whom they were named.[201] Dew ponds are now disappearing as regulations now require a mains water supply for cattle, though several have been or are being restored to encourage the local newt population. Indeed a new one was constructed in 2007 in the field at the top of Lathkill Dale, near the toilets.

In 1836, the ancient system of tithes, whereby freeholders would pay one tenth of the output of their land to the Church for its upkeep, was replaced by one based on a valuation of the affected land. (The village glebe, land formerly held by the Church itself, was exempt.) Commissions were established by the Tithe Commutation Act of 1836 to identify and value the affected land. As with the Enclosure Acts this resulted in a series of Tithe Awards. (The Monyash Tithe Award and Map can be viewed in the Derbyshire Records Office in Matlock.) By a series of Acts of Parliament stretching into the 1930s, the fixed tithe amounts were converted into annual sums charged on the affected land. With inflation these sums gradually diminished in value. Ultimately legislation was passed which commuted the annual charge into a single overall amount which, on payment, meant that the affected land was no longer subject to any payment.

Figure 48 Aerial picture showing some of the strip fields around Monyash. The red lines show the edges of the ancient field system with the larger fields created from the common land beyond. Photograph by Rob Faulkner. Copyright, and reproduced with the kind permission of, Rob Faulkner.

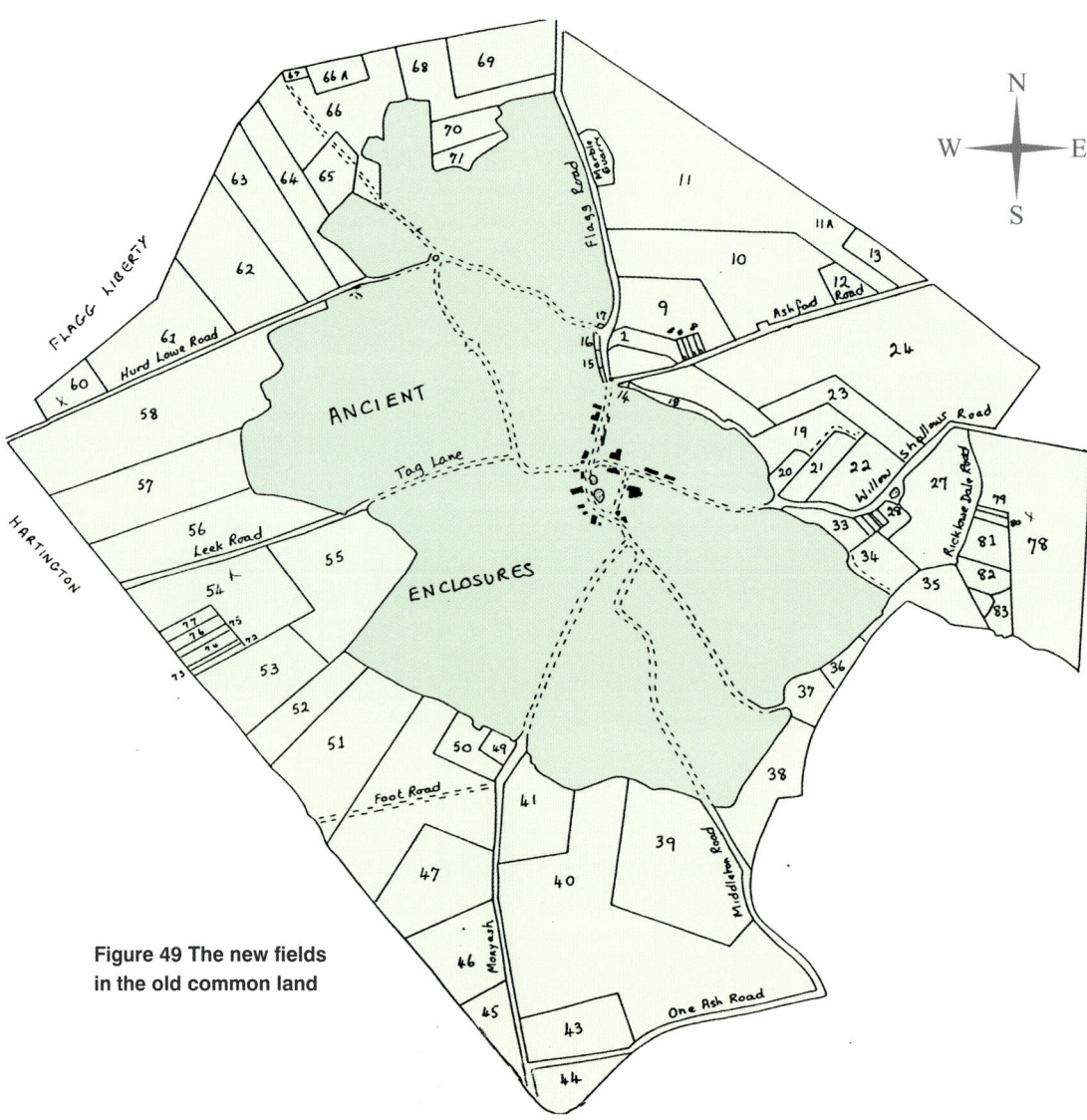

Figure 49 The new fields in the old common land

Box 21: The Monyash Enclosure Act 1771

There were about 5,000 individual Enclosure (or more correctly Inclosure) Acts in England between 1750 and 1860 resulting in over 21 per cent of the land in the country being 'enclosed'. In Monyash approximately 800 acres was enclosed and hundreds of miles of dry stone walls constructed as a result of the Monyash Enclosure Act 1771.

The commissioners appointed by the Act were John Beighton of Hazlewood, Thomas Harpur of Etwall and John Renshaw of Bakewell.[202] Their award, The Monyash Enclosure Award, allocated the newly enclosed land, shown in Figure 49, as follows:

Ann Cheney	35 37 57 83 1 11 18 24	Henry Bowman	6
	46 49 51 62 56 82	Joseph Brassington	20
Lord Scarsdale	27 38 39 41 55	William Ensor	63 79
John Gisborne	10 15	Peter Flint	69
George Goodwin	26 54 58 60 80	John Handley	29
Mary Roades	9 16 17 34 36 47 48	Ralph Handley	5
Rev Robert Charlesworth	52 68	Simon Handley	2
John Allsopp and Francis Fletcher	21 33 53	Thomas Handley	3
Ann Cheney and George Goodwin	25	Thomas Houlme	50
Sarah Needham and Ann Goodwin	40 45	Thomas Inglevany	75
Rev Peter Walthal and Thomas Brides		John Johnson	76
(as trustees for the poor of Bakewell)	23	Rev Robert Lomas	19
Dean and Chapter of Lichfield		George Longden	66
(in lieu of tithes)	78	Thomas Millward	14
Trustees of Monyash School	22	Daniel Morewood	77
Daniel Alcock	72	John Melland	59 61 81
Samuel Allen	67	George Newton	43 44
John Allwood	4	John Webster	29
Benjamin Ball	7	Richard Webster	64
Emma Ball	74	Isaac Wheeldon	70
Mary Bampton	28	John Wheeldon	71
Samuel Barker	56	Ralph Wheeldon	31
Thomas Boam	12	Thomas Wilde	73
George Boden	8	Jane Wilkinson	66A
William Bonsall	32		

24. TURNPIKES

The late 17th and early 18th centuries saw the arrival of the Turnpike roads (and the first use of the term road). Turnpikes were well constructed roads with stone foundations often laid with cobbles (later tarmac) on top. They had drainage channels and were usually walled to ensure the traffic went past the toll booths. Toll booths were erected along the turnpikes to collect taxes for the road's upkeep from the passing traffic. The idea was that as soon as the roads were in good repair the tolls could be removed. This did not happen, due to the continual need for expensive road maintenance and repairs, until 1888 when the responsibility for maintaining roads was passed to local authorities.

Monyash had at least two toll collecting houses when it was on the Newcastle-under-Lyme to Hassop turnpike (which went along Tagg Lane then Horse Lane – see Figure 50). Toll Bar House, the tiny house at the bottom of hill on the road towards Flagg and Taddington, was one and the other was the disused building at the end of Cross Lane by the bend in the main road (see Figure 28). One local is reputed to have been so annoyed at having to pay twice to go through his own village that he bought land at the side of one of them so he could avoid it.

Starting around 1724, the London-Derby-Manchester Turnpike was one of the first roads in the Peak District to be 'turnpiked', though it no longer followed the route of the Roman road from Derby. This new route from Derby came via Ashbourne, then not via Fenny Bentley as the current A515, but via Mapleton, then to Newhaven and Parsley Hay to The Bull i' th' Thorn, which was then a well-placed coaching inn (see Figure 50). The Bull i' th' Thorn was originally called Hurdlow House and the crossroads here called Hurdlow Thorn. (In the Middle Ages thorn trees were often planted to signify a crossroads or a change in direction of the road.)

The northern part of the Turnpike from Hurdlow to Buxton was improved around 1749 when the road was laid in parallel to the Roman road for much of the length between the Duke of York and Buxton.

The route from Ashbourne changed its direction around 1777 via Fenny Bentley (the current A515), when it was turnpiked with toll gates at Sandybrook and New Inns. The use of this new turnpike decreased when the Ashbourne to Leek road became a turnpike and linked up with Manchester via Macclesfield and Hazel Grove.

As a result of the turnpikes some of the older tracks, particularly those over rough ground and steep hills, started to fall into disuse as the better paved turnpikes were more suited to horses and carts, wagons and mail coaches. A detailed map by F Sichey Hall in 1852 (see Figure 50) shows that much of the old Roman road (part of it built on the Neolithic trackway) was no longer in use. (It also shows the rerouted A515 and also the recently opened Cromford & High Peak Railway – see Chapter 28.) Today, the only parts of the old Roman road between Buxton and Minninglow that remain in use are the half mile stretch of the A515 between the Duke of York and The Bull i' th' Thorn, and one mile of track near Pikehall. The short stretch from Bull i' th' Thorn to Benty Grange continued as a track until the 1950s.

Figure 50 F Sichey Hall's map of 1852

25. MONYASH AT ITS PEAK

In the middle of the 19th century Monyash was a busy place, with a population almost twice what it is today. By 1851 the population of Monyash had reached its peak at 473 inhabitants. During the first half of the 19th century the average number of people per house was around five. Since then it has declined to its current low of 1.9 people per dwelling (see Figure 51 and the Box 22: The Population of Monyash 1662-2008).

Box 22: The Population of Monyash 1662-2010

Date	Population	Dwellings	People per dwelling
1662	208e	52[205]	4.0
1670	235e	56[206]	4.2
1789	265e	53[207]	5.0
1801	330	66	5.0
1811	316	60	5.3
1821	381	78	4.9
1831	409	84	4.9
1841	435	90	4.8
1846	434	c92[208]	4.7
1851	473	98	4.8
1857	473	c103[209]	4.6
1861	460	94	4.9
1871	406	86	4.7
1881	399	89	4.5
1891	402	87	4.6
1901	349	86	4.1
1911	341	92	3.7
1921	350	88	4.0
1931	347	90	3.9
1951	318	93	3.4
1961	300	102	2.9
1971	302	105	2.9
1981	271	116[210]	2.3
1991	283	118e	2.4
1997	270	120[211]	2.3
2010	280	145e	1.9

Ten yearly figures are taken from the Census data

e = estimated from the number of houses or from the population figures

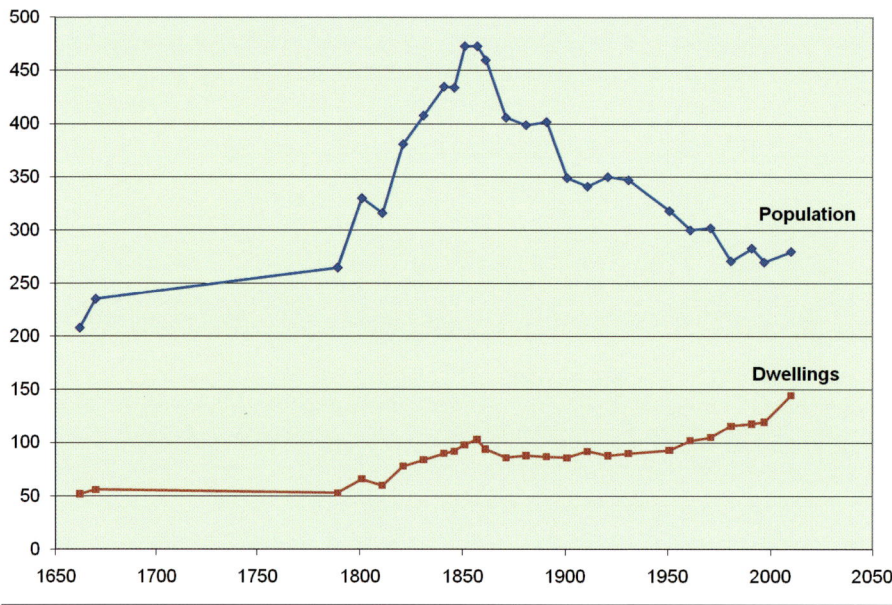

Figure 51 Population of Monyash and number of dwellings 1662-2010

The villagers depended chiefly upon farming, limestone quarrying and lead mining and there were many local tradespersons supporting these industries. Monyash was a small, almost self-sufficient community and, in the 19th century, provided a wide range of services including blacksmiths (see Figure 52), cobblers (see Figure 53), butchers, wheelwrights, wool merchants, inn keepers, joiners, dressmakers, shoe makers and even a 'rope-walk' making ropes for mining and farming and also for hauling boats on the canals. Box 23: Monyash Tradespersons – 1846 provides some of the names of the people doing these and other jobs. (Although there were about 20 people involved in lead mining including William Hibbert, the Methodist minister in 1861, lead mining is not included in the list because it presumably was not considered to be a trade.)

Joshua Millington, marble mason and quarry owner, was also a Primitive Methodist local preacher. The 1881 census shows him married to his wife, Sarah, from Youlgreave, who looked after the Chapel in Monyash. In 1881 they were aged 74 and 73 (see Box 17: Methodists and Monyash).[203]

In the mid 1980s cheese making provided a good income for some farms. For Rake End Farm (now Manor House) sales of cheese accounted for around 25 per cent of their income with the sale of cows, pigs, sheep and wool making up most of the rest. Their main outgoing was rent, just over 50 per cent of their income.

In addition to the 1846 list, Kelly's Directory of 1891 provides a few other working activities in the village including William Palfreyman who not only was a butcher and grocer but also ran the post office. Indeed his descendants continued to do so until it closed in 1996. There was also a coal merchant, John Hibbert and a stonemason, Edwin Johnson. Thomas Harrison was a farmer and chandler (candle maker) and on the night of the census a visiting primitive Methodist minister from Cornwall was staying with him.

The one-roomed school must have been overflowing in 1891 with 103 children, though the average attendance was only 70, some of whom were educated for free. Mr John Jones Morgan was headmaster and Mrs Mary Ann Morgan was the infant class mistress. Rev William Henry Ford was listed as the vicar at the time.[204]

The village had just (!) three pubs, The Bull's Head, The Golden Lion (see Figure 54) and The Bull i' th' Thorn (called The Bull's Head at Hurdlow which had recently changed its name from Hurdlow House).

Figure 52 The smithy circa 1910

Box 23: Monyash Tradespersons − 1846[212]

Earthenware dealer	Thomas Barker
Shoemaker	Thomas Bunting
Cattle dealer	Samuel Buxton
Beerhouse	Benjamin Froggatt
Schoolmaster	Thomas Green
Marble mason and quarry owner	Joshua Millington
Butcher	William Morewood
Priest	Rev Henry Charles Smith
Blacksmiths	John Bramwell William White
Wheelwrights	Anthony Bentley John Mortin
Rope maker	Thomas Pearce
Wool merchant	James Briddon
Shopkeepers	John Morewood Joseph Skidmore
Inns and Taverns	Robert Bagshaw (Bull's Head) William Needham (Bull i' th' Thorn) John Smith (Golden Lion)
Farmers	Samuel Ashmore Robert Bagshaw William Bagshaw Francis Blackwell Richard Bonsall (The Rake) Henry Bowman (One Ash Grange) John Bowman (Summerhill) Joseph Brassington James Briddon Samuel Briddon (and wool merchant) James Dunn Richard Finney Paul Gill (Endmore) Thomas Handley John Housley Thomas Housley John Melland Thomas Naylor Thomas Needham John Palfreyman Joseph White Joseph Wood

Figure 53 The centre of Monyash and the cobbler's workshop circa 1910
The small cobbler's workshop is just above the man on the left and was in use until the 1940s. To the left of it, side on, is another workshop, with cowshed behind, which were demolished when the road was widened around 1957.

Figure 54 Cottages on Church Street and The Golden Lion 1910
The Golden Lion is on the left and Wensley Terrace on the right where the houses, owned by the Bowman family of One Ash, were painted every year – the decorators can be seen wearing straw hats.

26. MONYASH – THE GRAND SALE

From the reign of William the Conqueror, Monyash was at times in the hands of the Crown or held by various lords of the manor beginning with Henry de Ferrers in 1066, later Robert de Salocia and Matthew de Aston, William de Lynford and William de Lynford Jr., eventually becoming part of the estate of the Earls of Shrewsbury. In the middle of the 17th century the 'manor' had been broken into several parts with several owners (See Box 12: Lords of the Manor of Monyash 1066-1721) though a good proportion had been purchased by the Cheney family in the early 18th century.

By 1861, having passed down through several generations of Cheneys, their part of Monyash was in the hands of Robert Henry Cheney (see Box 18: The Cheney Family). Other landowners included Thomas Bridden, Richard Finney, George Dunn, The Duke of Devonshire, John Melland and Henry Bowman.

Robert Cheney was a bachelor and was living in great style in Shropshire and appears to have had little interest in his land or his tenants in Monyash. On Monday 17th October 1861 he put the 'manor' of Monyash up for sale in 27 lots (see Figure 55). The lots included over 200 fields, several plantations, farms and cottages, The Bull's Head Inn (together with its stables, barn, brew house, cow yard, garden and yards), the wheelwright's shop, butcher's shop, limestone quarries (including Ricklow Quarry) and lead mines.

The sale particulars contained the following description: "Dairy farms for which the district is celebrated, and partly accommodation lands, and dispersed through the Township of Monyash, on the verge of good roads and approaches in every direction. The vicinity is to be appreciated for grouse shooting and other field sports; the general aspect of the country is agreeably undulated, highly picturesque, and the air salubrious". The selling agents also displayed some degree of optimism as they also mentioned that "a station will shortly be erected at Taddington, three miles from the Estate, on the extension of the Ambergate, Matlock, and Rowsley Railway to Buxton, now in the course of construction, and which will connect the district with London and Manchester". The station at Taddington never arrived but stations at Hurdlow and Parsley Hay were built on a different line (see the Box 26: The Cromford and High Peak Railway).

This Grand Sale gave other landowners, and also for the first time since they had been seized by William the Conqueror in 1066, the tenants themselves the opportunity to purchase their land and their houses.

It is believed some of the lots were bought by the Finney family of Flagg Hall, Flagg. Kelly's Directory of 1891 stated that the principal landowners were William Finney, now claiming to be Lord of the Manor, Stephen Melland and the trustees of the late Richard Finney.[213] Some villagers also bought small pieces of land and some cottages and businesses, for example, Thomas Finney of Blackedge Farm, Monyash bought The Bull's Head and some other pieces of land, William Hawley and Thomas Peter bought the land they were farming, and Thomas Housley of Knotlow also bought land in the village.[214] However, any investment by villagers or local landowners may well have become a problem as the economic boom was at an end. While farming, in particular sheep farming, continued to be the mainstay of the population, between 1851 and 1881 the population reduced from 473 to 399. The number of people involved in lead mining dropped from 20 in 1851 to just five by 1891 though many of the individuals moved into limestone and marble quarrying.[215]

In 1883 the pinfold was constructed. This is a small walled pound where stray animals were kept until they could be collected by their owners, on payment of a fine. The pinfold can still be seen at the end of the village on the road towards Flagg and Taddington.

DERBYSHIRE.

IN MONYASH.

PARTICULARS OF AN EXTENSIVE

FREEHOLD ESTATE

CONSISTING OF SEVERAL

DAIRY FARMS AND GROWING PLANTATIONS,

COMPRISING ALTOGETHER

FIVE HUNDRED AND FORTY-TWO ACRES, TWO ROODS, AND SEVEN PERCHES,

WITH SUITABLE

Farm Houses, Commodious Inn, a number of detached Inclosures for Accommodation Purposes, Cottages, and

VALUABLE AND EXTENSIVE MARBLE QUARRIES,

In the occupation of a highly respectable Tenantry, and most advantageously situate 7 miles from Buxton, 5 from Bakewell, Hartington, and Longnor, and 3 from Taddington, together with the

MANOR OF MONYASH AFORESAID,

Which will be Sold by Auction, by

MESSRS. MOODY AND NEWBOLD,

AT THE RUTLAND ARMS HOTEL, IN BAKEWELL,

ON THURSDAY, THE 17th DAY OF OCTOBER, 1861,

AT ONE FOR TWO O'CLOCK P.M. PRECISELY.

In Twenty-seven Lots, and subject to such Conditions as will be then produced.

William Hawley, of Monyash, will show the Estates, by permission of the Tenantry, and Particulars with Plans may be obtained of the Auctioneers, Wardwick, Derby; of Mr. William Goodwin, Tissington, near Ashbourne; of Mr. John Parkin, Estate Agent and Surveyor, Idridgehay, near Wirksworth; and of Messrs. Simpson and Taylor, Solicitors, Derby.

Figure 55 Monyash – The Grand Sale 1861

Box 24: Monyash Marble

Marble is polished limestone and the 'mottled grey marble' found in the Monyash area has a high content of fossilised crinoids. It is particularly attractive after polishing and is often used for ornamental purposes. Some of the limestone, particularly from Ricklow Quarry, owned by Henry Watson from 1742, was carted to the marble-works in Ashford-in-the-Water for cutting and polishing. These marble-works, built by Henry Watson in 1748 with the encouragement of his father Samuel, were the first of their kind ever established in Great Britain. Henry was also the inventor of the earliest Peak District cutting and polishing machine. The works were especially famous for Ashford 'black marble' with a high bitumen content which turns black when cut and polished. Large underground black marble mines are located near the west end of Ashford.[216]

The black marble columns in the Chapel at Chatsworth are believed to have come from Hardrake (Once a Week) Quarry. It is suggested that Black Ashford Marble can be found either side of the tomb of Bess of Hardwick and that the tomb of Queen Elizabeth I is also made of black marble.

The lighter stone from Monyash has been used for the floors, stairs and fireplaces in many public buildings and fine houses in Britain including Chatsworth House.[217] An example can be seen in the village, the flag stones in the entrance to The Bull's Head.

The marble-works in Ashford closed in 1905 though Hardrake (Once a Week) Quarry on the outskirts of the village continues, occasionally. (See Chapter 15: Monyash Mines and Quarries.)

27. THE FIRST CHURCH RESTORATION

By the late 19th century the south porch of the Church had fallen down (see Figure 41) and the north transept had disappeared.

In 1886 the inside of the Church would have looked rather different from how it does today (see Figure 56). It had a number of box pews of different sizes capable of seating about 150 people. These pews, together with the reader's desk and a pulpit, had been installed in 1841. There was space for an organ in the south transept though just prior to 1886 a harmonium was in place in the chancel against the north wall. The whole area between the south and north doors was partitioned off from the rest of the Church. A disused gallery existed above the middle third of the closed off area by the tower and a staircase led up to it from the north-west corner of the north aisle. Heating the Church was a problem then, as it is now, and there were two stoves, one in the middle of the aisle between the pews and a second by the south door. On the north side of the chancel arch was a prayer desk and the 15th century octagonal font was situated in the middle of the chancel.

Between 1886 and 1888 there was a major programme of restoration of St Leonard's Church. This was brought about by, and chiefly at the expense of, Archdeacon Edward Balston, vicar of Bakewell.[218] The Rev Dr Edward Balston (1817-1891), formerly the headmaster of Eton, was vicar of Bakewell from 1869 to 1891. He was the Rural Dean and Archdeacon from 1873. He also commissioned Alfred

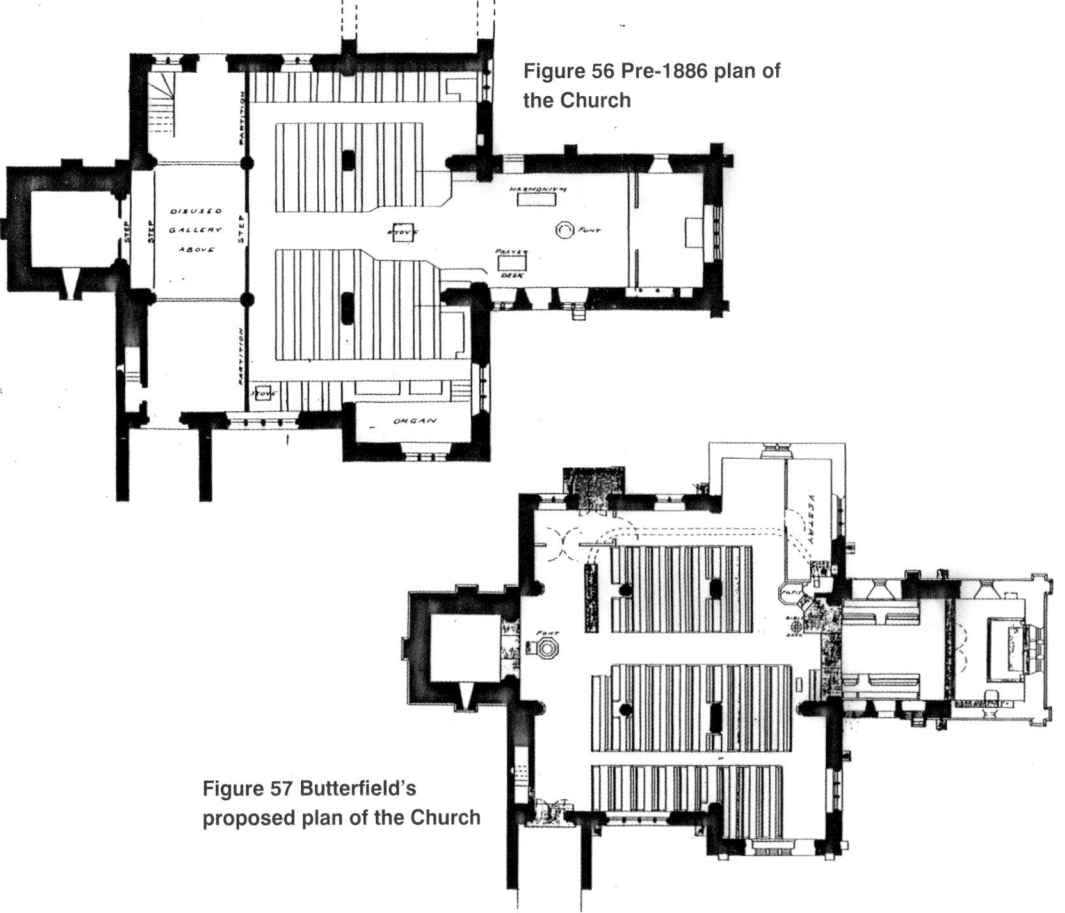

Figure 56 Pre-1886 plan of the Church

Figure 57 Butterfield's proposed plan of the Church

Waterhouse to design a new Bakewell vicarage which he paid for himself. He was also responsible for embellishing the chancel of Bakewell Church.[219]

The restoration of St Leonard's was carried out by the renowned London architect William Butterfield (1814-1900) and it remains an important example of his work (see Box 25: The Butterfield Restoration 1886-1888). Butterfield was responsible for the restoration of many churches in Derbyshire, including Hathersage, which he restored between 1849 and 1852. His work was usually commissioned by the Rev Henry Cottingham. Monyash was one of his later restorations. This work appears to be the only one of his projects not to be supported by the patronage of Cottingham.[220]

St Leonard's priest, the Rev John Foulger, had been instrumental in planning the restoration, but was no longer in post at the start of the project. The lack of a priest appears to have been used as an excuse not to get a faculty to undertake the works. The arrival of the Rev Charles Isaac Bickerstaff towards the end of 1886 led to an application being made in early 1887.

William Butterfield oversaw a considerable amount of work including the rebuilding of the north transept, the spire and much of the chancel (see Figure 57). The chancel, nave and aisles were re-roofed and the interior partly stripped out and new tiles, pews, and plain glass windows inserted (see Box 25: The Butterfield Restoration 1886-1888).

Box 25: The Butterfield Restoration 1886-1888

The first task of this major restoration was emergency work to take down the spire and make safe the tower walls. The spire was rebuilt in the original style using most of the old materials. It was noted that there was a crack "from top to bottom" in the tower.[221] It is not clear whether this work was supervised by Butterfield.

Butterfield however did oversee some considerable building works. Extensive work was undertaken in the chancel, including the complete rebuilding of the north and east walls from their foundations. The new stone work is noticeable because it is evenly coursed, unlike the older roughly coursed stone work. The shallow-pitched roof of the chancel and nave were removed and replaced with a steep-pitched roof using scissor-braced trusses, taking them back to their pre 15th century height. The old square-headed window in the east end of the chancel was replaced with a new three light window. The priest's door was rebuilt with a 'Caernarfon' arch (a flat-topped 'arch' with rounded shoulders – see Figure 58) whereas a more simple design had probably existed before. The door was blocked up. Butterfield also installed marble shafts in the sedilia, which have since been replaced with the original stone work. The foliage on the north corbel was repaired.

Previously the floor throughout the church was level and so Butterfield added one step into the chancel and a further step into the sanctuary at the far end of the chancel.

The foundations of the north transept were uncovered and a new transept was built on the old lines containing what was presumably the original medieval window. The north transept roof structure matches the roof structure over the nave, whereas the south transept roof has arched rafters forming a barrel vault.[222]

The double-pitched slate roofs on the north and south aisles were removed and replaced with shallow, mono-pitched, lean-to roofs covered with lead. The south porch had only one side wall standing. Butterfield rebuilt the porch with a shallow-pitched, leaded roof. An oak screen was constructed on the outer wall of the south porch. The font was moved from the chancel to the back of the nave.

Figure 58 The Caernarfon Arch

Butterfield removed the screens that split the nave and separated off the west end of the nave and removed the gallery above the middle of this area (see Figures 56 and 57), and the steps leading up to it from the north door. He closed off the tower arch with a screen and created an inner lobby for the north door, and a screened-off vestry in the north transept. (The oak screen that we see today around the Lady Chapel (south transept) was fitted somewhat later – see Chapter 34). A new, oak door was fitted in the south doorway. All the internal walls were covered in cement render.

Little of the internal fabric of the pre-restoration Church remains. In keeping with the trend to bring more powerful, emotional symbolism and energy to churches (the Oxford Movement) Butterfield re-laid the nave and aisle floors with terracotta and yellow tiles. Yellow and blue encaustic tiles were laid in the reredos (the ornamental screens covering the walls either side of the altar), to form chevrons. The Rev Thomas Watson, priest from 1938 to 1953, disliked them so much that at the Parochial Church Council meeting on the 24th April 1940, he asked for them to be covered by curtains. They remain covered up today. The Church was furnished with pine pews (the old box pews were removed), oak choir stalls, an oak pulpit on a stone base and a lectern, all in a style associated with Butterfield.[223]

The cost of this restoration was between £3,000 and £4,000 and the Church was re-opened by the Bishop of Southwell on 9th May 1888.[224]

28. DECLINING TRAFFIC AND THE REMOVAL OF TOLLS

Three events were to reduce the traffic on parts of the Derby to Manchester turnpike. One was the opening of the Nottingham to Newhaven turnpike around 1759, allowing a faster route to/from London down the Via Gellia to Cromford and then Derby. This route was shorter by around five miles.

Secondly, the northern stretch between Brierlow Bar and Buxton was also affected. Before 1810 the traffic from Buxton to Ashford and Bakewell came down the Derby turnpike to Brierlow Bar, then via Chelmorton to Ashford. In 1810 a route was opened that followed the river south of Buxton to Ashford (which later became the A6).

The third was the coming of the railways. In the early-to-mid 19th century the railways started to link major and minor centres of population and F Sichey Hall's map (see Figure 50) also shows the new Cromford and High Peak Railway (see Box 26: The Cromford and High Peak Railway) passing close to Monyash at Parsley Hay (the southern junction of the Monyash Road with the A515) and Hurdlow, half a mile from The Bull i' th' Thorn (see Figures 59 and 60).

The arrival of rail travel was an efficient way of transporting goods and a much more comfortable way of moving people than by stage coach. As a result there was a significant reduction in toll takings and this form of taxation was eventually abandoned by the government in 1888 when the responsibility for maintaining roads was passed to local authorities.

Figure 59 Hurdlow railway station April 1929
The train is thought to have been a special train bringing visitors to Flagg Races on the Tuesday after Easter
Photograph by Dr John R Hollick. Copyright C M & J M Bentley. Reproduced with the kind permission of Michael Bentley.

Figure 60 Parsley Hay railway station June 1962
Photograph by Harry Townley. Copyright C M & J M Bentley. Reproduced with the kind permission of Michael Bentley

Box 26: The Cromford and High Peak Railway

Running close to the western boundary of the Parish of Monyash was the Cromford and High Peak Railway (C&HPR). This was one of the world's first long-distance railways. It was also the steepest and had the sharpest curve on the network. The railway was built to join two canals, the Cromford Canal at Cromford (an extension of the Erewash Canal that linked to the River Trent) and the Peak Forest Canal at Whaley Bridge. Its purpose was to plug a gap in the national waterway network and link the coalfields of Nottinghamshire and Derbyshire with the developing industries around Manchester. Canals were the main method of goods transportation of the day and so a trans-peak waterway was originally considered in the 1820s, but it was too difficult a task at an estimated cost of £650,000. Josiah Jessop, whose father had built the Cromford Canal, designed and built a railway instead, a much cheaper option at just £150,000. The planning for the railway began in 1824, before steam locomotives were widely in use[225] and it was designed, and operated, like a canal with flat sections linked by long gradients (equivalent to flights of locks) with individual operators leasing their wagons and drawing them by horse.[226]

The line took five years to construct and was completed in 1831, initially using short cast iron rails (still visible at Middleton Top) laid on stone blocks.

It was a significant feat of engineering going across the high White Peak plateau and over the Pennines. This 33 mile line started at Cromford at a height of 84 metres (277 feet) and ascended rapidly to around 300 metres (984 feet) at Middleton Top near Wirksworth. The railway then ran downhill past Hopton and Longcliffe before a long slow rise to Brundcliffe at over 300 metres, south west of Monyash, then down to Parsley Hay and Hurdlow, where there was a level crossing, on past Hindlow Quarry, curving steeply upwards and westwards at Harpur Hill, past what is now the Industrial Estate, before going due north to the west of Burbage and its summit by the tunnel near Ladmanlow, through the Pennines, at 386 metres (1,266 feet) to Wildmoor, then off on a long descent along the Goyt Valley to Whaley Bridge at 157 metres (517 feet). Because of the steep inclines, including gradients of 1 in 7, the railway required a total of seven stationary steam engines (four at the Cromford end and three at the Whaley Bridge end) to pull wagons up the steep slopes. The stationary engine at Hopton was later removed as more powerful trains, 'double heading', could just manage to pull their loads up the steep 1 in 14 gradient – this was the steepest 'normal' railway line in the UK with trains sometimes having to take several runs at it. This railway also included one of the sharpest curves on the whole of the rail network, the Gotham Curve, half a mile south west of Pikehall.

Until 1833 horses were used to move the wagons along the more level sections of the railway with wagons taking two days to travel from one end of the railway to the other. However, around 1833, the first of the C&HPR's locomotives arrived on the scene. It had been built at Robert Stephenson & Co's works and was named 'Peak', possibly working between the Middleton Top and Hopton Bottom inclines.[227] The next two engines arrived in 1835 and were built by Edward Bury & Co of Liverpool.[228]

From 1856 to 1877 a limited passenger service operated on the C&HPR line from Cromford initially terminating at Ladmanlow (where Grin Low Road meets the A53 Leek road just past Burbage) with a connecting bus service for the mile into the centre of Buxton. An 1856 timetable shows stations at Cromford, Steeplehouse, Middleton, Hopton, Longcliffe, Friden, Hurdlow (on the outskirts of Monyash), Hindlow and Ladmanlow. At this time the stations were little more than sheds, often without name boards and usually some distance from the village they purported to serve.[229] More stations had opened by 1874, including Parsley Hay, when the passenger service went all the way to Whaley Bridge. However there was only one train in each direction each day and the passenger carriage was attached to the rear of a goods train; the passengers were required to walk up the steep inclines and the whole journey took almost a full day. The 1874 timetable shows the 11.45 train from Cromford arriving in Whaley Bridge at 17.10 and the Whaley Bridge to Cromford train setting off at 9.20 and arriving at 14.45 (see Figure 61). The passenger service did not last long.

This impressive feat of engineering was completed around 30 years before the Midland Railway line from Derby to Manchester was built along the Wye valley. Unfortunately, it was doomed to failure and experienced financial difficulties almost from the start. Canals had formed the main heavy transportation network in the UK, and this railway was part of that network, joining two canals together. However it was to be the railways themselves that would quickly become the main means of transporting heavy goods. One such railway was built from Ashbourne to Buxton, using part of the C&HPR, joining it just south of Parsley Hay close to Monyash (see Box 27: The London and North Western Railway Company). The C&HPR was taken over by the LNWR in March 1861 and continued limited freight operations. The section of the line between Middleton Top and Cromford (with the long Middleton Incline) closed in 1963 with the rest of the line finally closing in October 1967. The track bed of the C&HPR was turned into the High Peak Trail in 1971 (see Box 28: Cycle Trails).

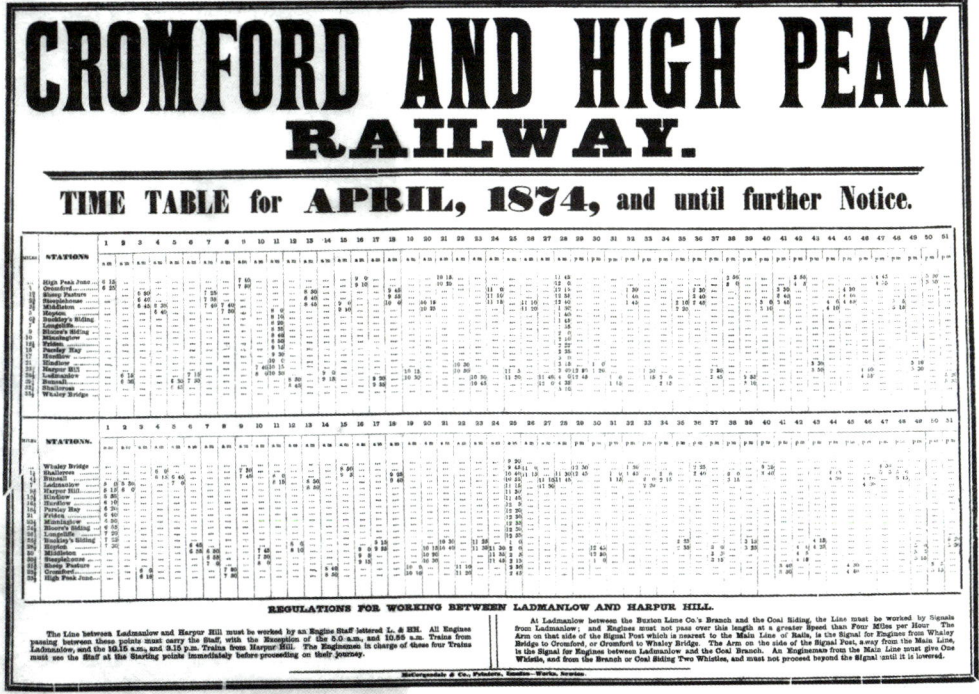

Figure 61 C&HPR's 1874 timetable

29. HARDSHIPS

For most people in the early 20th century, calling out the doctor was a great expense, so many working people in Monyash, like elsewhere, took out a form of insurance to help cover the costs. Monyash Friendly Benefit Society, one of many across the country, was established on the 16th June 1849 and was an important institution before the introduction of the welfare state and the National Health Service. The Society provided villagers with some income in case of sickness and entitled villagers to use the services of doctors and also the Cottage Hospital in Bakewell (Bakewell War Memorial Cottage Hospital, now a nursing home). Subscriptions were one shilling (5p) per month. (A photograph of the Society's banner is shown in Figure 62.)

The two World Wars (1914-1918 and 1939-1945) brought hardships to the village, including shortages of food, machinery and manpower as fit young men left the village to join the war effort, some of them never to return.

Shortly after the First World War, a war memorial was erected by the people of Monyash on the village green. This three metre high pillar on a stone base surrounded by a chain commemorates the 47 people from the village who fought in the First World War, 13 of whom died in the conflict. The monument was later inscribed with the names of those who fought in the Second World War, where 17 villagers served with one dying. The inscription reads, "In honour of those who nobly served their country and the undying memory of the gallant lives laid down." A separate memorial plaque was placed in the Lady Chapel of the Church (see Chapter 34).

During the Great Depression of the 1930s there were severe hardships and a great shortage of jobs and money. (The Great Depression was a western world financial crisis following a stock market crash in 1929. It had a devastating effect on the UK; construction was virtually halted, farmers suffered as

crop prices plummeted and personal incomes fell. Many people were hit very hard.) Monyash Friendly Society provided an important safety net for many people in the village. The Society met in The Golden Lion until it closed (around 1919) and then moved to a room above the bar in The Bull's Head. The Friendly Society was disbanded on the introduction of the National Health Service in 1948.[230]

The Methodists also supported people during difficult times, including running outings and events. Picnics were held at Summerhill Farm and there were trips to Wirksworth Park by motor bus and even trips to Blackpool from Hurdlow Station (see Box 26: The Cromford and High Peak Railway).[231]

Figure 62 Friendly Society banner

30. MODERN CONVENIENCES

While the turnpikes and railways arrived in the 18th and 19th centuries, 'modern conveniences', like the motor car, mains water and electricity did not arrive until the 20th century.

Most trades relied on horses and carts to move their goods and, to deal with the bad weather, Monyash even had its own horse-drawn snow plough in the first half of the 20th century. During the famously bad winter of 1947 it was hitched to a tractor but it made little impact on the huge snowdrifts that isolated the village from Bakewell for weeks.

It is believed that the first person to own a car in the village, around 1918, was Rev John Fawcett Warden. He was blind and employed a driver to take him round his parish.

Figure 63 Car leading the Friendly Society procession 1918

Photograph courtesy of the Peak Advertiser

At the same time a car, possibly the Rev Warden's, headed the procession of the Monyash Friendly Benefit Society on the occasion of their annual feast. This took place on the Wednesday in Whit week each year and the procession began at The Bull's Head, went round the village, stopping at the Church for the service, then returning to The Bull's Head for refreshments. Figure 63 shows the car outside the smithy and Bull's Head leading the procession, which included the Birchover band (see also Figure 64). (Whitsuntide is a Christian festival observed on the seventh Sunday after Easter. This has transformed into what is now called the Late Spring Bank Holiday held on the last Monday in May. Although this is not the Church's Whitsuntide, it is often referred to as Whit Monday.)

Since Neolithic times villagers drew their drinking water from the wells around the village, despite the likelihood they were tainted with lead. (The meres were not used for drinking water but were used for watering animals and for non-drinking purposes, such as washing clothes.) The wells were no longer needed when mains water was finally piped into the village in 1935.

Figure 64 Friendly Society procession circa 1918

The picture shows an earlier version of the banner than in Figure 62

The first telephone was available for use at Monyash post office at some time during the late 1920s. It had been possible to send a 'telegraph' message for some years previously. Electricity arrived in the 1930s. Until that time schools, workplaces and houses were lit with oil lamps and candles. Electricity was not welcomed by everyone; many people were frightened of it and refused to have it for some time. It was installed in the Church in 1937 at a cost of £83, some years before it was installed in the vicarage.

Mains sewerage arrived much later, in the second half of the 20th century, with people using earth closets until then. (Earth closets were outside toilets, in a small well-ventilated shed, sometimes shared by several families. After use a layer of earth was used to cover the most recent contribution. Workers would come and empty the buckets into a cart on a regular basis. This would be taken away and be put in a 'compost heap' and later spread on the fields as a form of cheap fertiliser.)

31. CLOSURES

The 20th century was also a time of closures in Monyash. Resident Amy Fotherby described the village as she remembered it in 1919, when she arrived in Monyash as a new bride. When interviewed in 1975 at the age of 77, she recalled that the village had two smithies, two joiners, a butchers, a chandler, a doctor, a policeman, a candle factory, a lace factory and five pubs. She then witnessed the decline of the village over the following years.[232]

Around 1919 The Golden Lion pub closed its doors leaving The Bull's Head in the village and The Bull i' th' Thorn, near the village, as the only operating pubs. By the 1930s there were only a handful of shops; the cobblers at the far end of Handley Lane, the post office and general store, Millington's store (at Rock House) and what was then referred to as the new shop, the village store on Church Street (now called Ash Tree Cottage).

For some years the village had its own policeman stationed in The Croft. The 1911 census reports that PC Alfred Stanley and his family were in residence.[233] At a later date, maybe around 1920, the police house moved to Lea Hurst (now Lea House). This village facility ended with the outbreak of World War II in 1939.

In 1958 the last remaining lead mine, Magpie Mine, closed due to the high costs of extraction, the availability of cheaper imported lead and the replacement of lead by copper pipes. Some ten years later, in 1968, the last traditional Derbyshire lead miner and the last living link to the lead mining era, Charles Henry Millington, one time grand-juryman of the Barmote Court, died aged 90 at his home, Rock House, Monyash.[234] Although Magpie Mine and other mine workings are still visible today (see Chapter 15: Monyash Mines and Quarries) the lead mining era, going back to Roman times, if not earlier, was finally over.

Another industry that may have employed several villagers for over 100 years was the Cromford and High Peak Railway. By the early 20th century only a few freight trains used this line (see Box 26: The Cromford and High Peak Railway). The railway that took over C&HPR's line, including Parsley Hay and Hurdlow stations (the two stations close to Monyash), The London and North Western Railway Company, also probably employed a few villagers. The railway provided important services to the village; a passenger service to Buxton, Manchester and Ashbourne, a direct service to London, and the delivery of cattle feed and farm implements, for example, into the village, and for taking away milk and cheese from the farms (see Box 27: The London and North Western Railway Company). Hurdlow station closed to passengers in 1949, followed by Parsley Hay in 1954. The last freight train ran in 1967. (The track beds were later turned into cycle trails, see Box 28: Cycle Trails.)

The village also had its own Reading Room (reached via the outside stone steps by what is now called the Old Reading Room). This was a male preserve which provided a quiet place for reading the newspaper or the Bible, or playing cards or dominoes in the evenings. Gambling, alcohol and women were not allowed. With the increasing popularity of television the Reading Room closed sometime around 1960. A framed roll of honour listing the Reading Room's members who served and died in the First World War is now located in the Lady Chapel in St Leonard's Church.

At one time Monyash had its own petrol station and repair garage situated between the School playing field and Fere Mere, where Ashmere (the house) is now (see Figure 65). The garage closed in the late 1980s. In 1996 the village post office closed (see Figure 66). The last shop, the 'new shop', on Church Street followed ten years later in 2006 (see Figure 67).

Figure 65 Monyash garage circa 1965

Figure 66 Monyash post office circa 1950

With a building, cowshed and store, in the foreground that was knocked down around 1957 to accommodate road widening.

Figure 67 The 'new' shop on Church Street before its closure in 2006

Box 27: The London and North Western Railway Company

The mid 19th century was a time of intense competition between the railway companies. Two companies in particular were trying to set up railways from London to Manchester. The first company to succeed, via a rather circuitous route, was the London and North Western Railway Company (LNWR). It used North Staffordshire Railway's line to Ashbourne and then built a line from Ashbourne to Buxton then Manchester. (Buxton was also gaining popularity at the time as a spa resort.) A critical part of its plan was its acquisition, on a 999 year lease, in 1861 of the declining Cromford and High Peak Railway (C&HPR) (see Box 26: The Cromford and High Peak Railway). This gave it access to the route from Parsley Hay to Hindlow from where it would construct its line to Buxton, closing the C&HPR's Hindlow to Ladmanlow and Whaley Bridge line in the process.

The main reason for the construction of the railway was to take limestone out of the Peak District. There was heavy competition from other rail companies to move limestone. Until the opening of this railway, LNWR's only route to the south of England was north via Manchester. This new route also allowed it to offer an unrivalled five hour direct passenger service between London and Buxton.[235]

Building this branch of the LNWR was easier than the C&HPR but there were still many difficulties to overcome. It required several large cuttings, including the one that can be seen close to Parsley Hay. Large viaducts were also needed in Buxton; the most impressive is the one over Duke's Drive which is still used for quarry traffic from Dowlow. Double tracks were laid between Hindlow and Parsley Hay. Although wide enough for two tracks only a single track was laid from Parsley Hay to Ashbourne to reduce costs. LNWR built a junction just south of Parsley Hay where the line via Hartington and Tissington to Ashbourne forked from the Cromford line (see Figure 68). At the same time the original Parsley Hay station was moved from the north side of the road bridge to the south side to accommodate tracks into the goods yard.

The LNWR's main competitor for a route from London to Manchester, the Midland Railway, arrived in Buxton almost at the same time, with the two companies' lines terminating at different stations. LNWR's station is the current railway station. Midland Railway's was directly opposite, on the other side of the road, roughly where Spring Garden's Shopping Centre car park is today.

A limited service began operating in June 1884 between Buxton and Parsley Hay and the line was fully opened on 4th August 1899 running regular freight services and seven passenger services both ways between Buxton and Ashbourne, with carriages that continued onto London twice daily. When the LNWR's railway opened in 1899, Parsley Hay station, on the outskirts of Monyash, was one of the highest stations in England. The platforms were provided with new buildings (see Figure 60).

Although the areas the railway served, like Monyash, were sparsely populated, many people came to rely on the line for the delivery of foodstuffs, cattle-feed, seed and farm implements and also for taking cheese from Hartington and fresh milk away from the farms.[236]

However with the increasing popularity of car travel and the use of roads for heavy transportation, the line's decline was inevitable. The passenger service to Cromford stopped soon after LNWR opened the line to Ashbourne. The 'direct' London service was withdrawn in 1917. Hurdlow station closed in 1949 and the wooden station buildings were pulled down ten years later (see Figure 69). Regular passenger trains stopped in 1954 and the last freight train ran to Parsley Hay in 1967, though there were several passenger specials over the years with people being brought to Flagg Races or latterly just to travel on this stunningly picturesque line (see Figure 59). Parsley Hay station closed to passengers in 1954 and was demolished in 1964.[237] In 1971 the old track beds were turned into the Tissington and the High Peak Trails (see Box 28: Cycle Trails).

Figure 68 Parsley Hay station and junction in August 1953

Parsley Hay station centre with the goods yard bottom right (location of cycle hire now) and the junction beyond the station with lines splitting to Cromford and Ashbourne.

Photograph by Harry Townley. Copyright C M & J M Bentley. Reproduced with the kind permission of Michael Bentley.

Figure 69 Hurdlow Station August 1953

Photograph by Harry Townley. Copyright C M & J M Bentley. Reproduced with the kind permission of Michael Bentley.

32. RENAISSANCE AND REVIVAL

Despite the many closures during the 20th century, a revival was already well underway. In 1951 Monyash found itself at the centre of the first national park in England, the Peak District National Park. The Peak District National Park Authority was set up to work with local people and businesses to conserve and enhance the natural beauty, wildlife and cultural heritage of the area and to promote opportunities for the understanding and enjoyment of the Park's special qualities by the public. It was also required to provide for the social and economic needs of the local population.

In 1980 the village was designated as a Conservation Area within the National Park. Conservation areas recognise the special character, architecture, history or landscape of an area and this status made some buildings eligible for repair and restoration grants. The designation helped maintain the character of the village, for example unsightly electricity and telephone poles were removed and lines laid underground in the main part of the village. Strict controls were put in place for new buildings and for the colour and nature of replacement doors and windows.

A major investment in the village, and a key driver in the renaissance of the village, came along in the shape of the Integrated Rural Development (IRD) Scheme. Between 1981 and 1988 Monyash became, along with Longnor, a pilot for a new development scheme funded by the European Union. Monyash was designated as a 'Disadvantaged Area' and the IRD Scheme was a plan to find ways of reversing the decline in population, creating new business opportunities, increasing job opportunities and encouraging community initiatives while maintaining the environmental quality of the area.[238]

This project (led by Ken Parker from the Peak District National Park) appears to have been very successful judging by the improvements that have taken place since then. The cost of the Scheme (phase 1 – 1981-1984 and phase 2 – 1984-1988) was around £185,000, though the value of the work done was over £500,000 across the two villages. Involvement in the schemes was entirely voluntary and most of the work was carried out by the villagers.[239]

The Women's Institute hut on Church Street, a simple wooden building in great need of repair (see Figure 70), was replaced by a purpose built village hall which serves as a dining room and sports hall for the Primary School and is used for many other local events. The new village hall (see Figure 71) was opened in 1986 by the Duchess of Devonshire.

A children's play area (see Figure 72) was built by villagers in 1983-1984, on land behind The Bull's Head kindly leased by the owner. The play area, opened by Ken Parker (see Figure 73), won a Derbyshire Village Ventures prize in 1984. It was later demolished in 2006 to make way for an even better one, opened by the Dowager Duchess of Devonshire later that year (see Figure 74).

Also, as part of the IRD Scheme, the old toll bar cottage on the road to Flagg was saved from dereliction and the Quaker Chapel repaired. The old smithy was renovated to provide business premises, initially Tool Hire Bakewell, now the Smithy Café. Grants were provided to support the village shop and the development of several bed and breakfast accommodations. The churchyard benefited from tree planting, carried out by the Primary School children, ground levelling and shrub planting. Jack Mere car park was improved and an information board provided. The School playing field was renovated, street lighting installed and repairs made to the market cross and war memorial.

Agricultural improvement grants were also provided to maintain the miles of dry stone walls, provide water supplies to fields and renovate Dew ponds. Flower rich fields were developed and new woodland areas planted (see Box 31: Flora and Fauna).

Perhaps the most impressive achievement came in 1987 when, eager to improve the cramped conditions at the Primary School, the villagers raised most of the £50,000 required to provide an extra classroom and store, doing much of the work themselves (see Figure 75 and Box 19: Monyash Primary School). Money was raised and work was completed in 1989 and the new room (which, a hundred years ago, used to be the school master's house) was officially opened by the Duchess of Devonshire on 2nd September 1989 (see Figure 76).

The work of the IRD scheme attracted national and international recognition, in particular the Europa Nostra Award (the small stone at the pointed end of the village green) "for the admirable revitalisation of two small villages through the joint action of public agencies combined with local initiative and commitment" and a lot of local effort. The Europa Nostra award is the European Union Prize for Cultural Heritage. Its specific objectives are to promote, at a European level, high standards of quality in the fields of heritage conservation, architecture, urban and rural planning and to advocate a balanced and sustainable development of urban and rural, built and natural environment.[240] The Europa Nostra Award was presented to the village in 1986.

Around the same time the people of Monyash and the IRD scheme received the Council for the Protection of Rural England's merit award "in recognition for their contribution to the environment". The plaque is located on the wall by Jack Mere car park. This scheme, now called the Countryside Awards, recognises projects and initiatives that make a positive, visible contribution to the enhancement of the countryside.

Figure 70 The old WI hut circa 1980 which was replaced by the village hall[241] Copyright Peak District National Park Authority. Reproduced with the kind permission of the Peak District National Park Authority.

Figure 71 The village hall opened in 1986

Figure 72 The old play park 1984

Figure 73 Ken Parker at the opening of the children's play park in 1984
Picture published by courtesy of the Derbyshire Times.

Figure 74 The new play park 2006

Figure 75 Villagers working on the new classroom in 1989
Picture published by courtesy of the Derbyshire Times.

Figure 76 The completed classroom with the school children[242]
Photograph taken by Ray Manley. Copyright Peak District National Park Authority. Reproduced with the kind permission of the Peak District National Park Authority.

Box 28: Cycle Trails

In 1969 the Peak Park Planning Board and Derbyshire County Council bought two track beds from the London and North Western Railway (LNWR). One was the 17 mile stretch of the Cromford and High Peak Railway (C&HPR) (see Box 26: The Cromford and High Peak Railway) from Dowlow, near Buxton, to High Peak Junction, Cromford (which was owned by LNWR). The second was the old track bed of the LNWR's line from Parsley Hay to Ashbourne. The price was £1.

The two routes join at Parsley Hay. The route to Cromford became the High Peak Trail and the Ashbourne route was the Tissington Trail. Both trails, which opened in 1971, can be accessed close to where the old stations were at Parsley Hay and Hurdlow on the outskirts of Monyash. The cycle hire centre at Parsley Hay is sited on the old goods yard; the station was situated on the other side of the bridge. The trails are open all year round and used by walkers, cyclists and horse riders. Bikes can be hired at Parsley Hay. (The trail stops at Dowlow because the quarry still uses the northern part of the track bed to take limestone northwards via the old LNWR's line to Buxton and beyond.) Both trails are part of the National Cycle Network and form alternative starts to the 130 mile Pennine Bridleway to Hebden Bridge in West Yorkshire.

The High Peak Trail follows the route of the old Cromford and High Peak Railway, covering a mainly high level and scenic route 14 miles from Parsley Hay to the High Peak Junction, one mile south-east of the centre of Cromford. The route is reasonably level apart from a couple of very steep inclines after Middleton Top. Here is the restored Middleton Top Engine House which can sometimes be seen in action. The Tissington Trail goes downhill to Ashbourne, again about 14 miles. Hartington signal box, beside the Tissington Trail, has been converted into an Information Centre, and is open at weekends during the summer.

These two trails also join up with the trail around Carsington Water and the Manifold Track from Hulme End to Waterhouses. More information can be found at www.peakdistrict.gov.uk/cycle

33. A NEW SPIRIT OF COMMUNITY

Although the funding for the improvements ceased in 1988 many of the original projects became self-funding or self-sustaining. It could also be argued that the IRD Scheme provided impetus for many activities and projects since.

In 1985, in response to an appeal by St Leonard's Church for funds for a new renovation project (see next chapter), a small committee created the White Peak Walk.[243] The White Peak Walk is a 26 mile Challenge Walk around the hills and dales of the White Peak area of Derbyshire, starting and finishing in the village. It has been held every year in mid July (except in 2001, due to an outbreak of Foot and Mouth Disease). It is staffed by many villagers and friends and raises more than £1,000 each year for local good causes, including the Church and Chapel. It also pays for the Christmas tree on the green each year, around which villagers now meet to sing carols on Christmas Eve.

Another 'Monyash Institution', which began in 1995, is the annual Monyash Christmas, usually held on the Friday evening before Christmas day. This is a secular and well attended celebration in the Church with performances by locals, school children and other supporters.

In the early 1990s the land at Soldier's Croft, which is owned by the Ralph Rider Trust, was used to develop five houses as part of an affordable housing scheme for locals and their relatives. The houses were officially opened by HRH Princess Alexandra on the 19th October 1993.

Around the same time the Parish Council erected a bus shelter on the green. Although not welcomed by everyone, it is much appreciated by the children waiting for the morning bus to Lady Manners School and by walkers sheltering from the wind and rain waiting for the infrequent buses to Bakewell or Buxton.

Figure 77 VE Day street party 1995 outside The Bull's Head

In a new spirit of community, villagers celebrated the 50th anniversary of Victory in Europe (VE) Day in May 1995. Although it was a cool day a street party was held outside The Bull's Head; games were played on the village green and there was an exhibition of war time memorabilia in the village hall (see Figure 77).

In September 1997 the Parish Council had a new public toilet constructed conveniently at the head of Lathkill Dale, just outside the village. This allowed for the removal of the unsightly block that had been situated at the edge of the School's playing field for some years.

In 2000 the Millennium tree was planted on the village green joining the 'king' and 'queen' trees, planted to celebrate the coronation of King George V and Queen Mary in 1911. The Millennium tree (the tree closest to the post box and the old post office) was donated by Derbyshire Dales District Council. At its base is a plaque with the names of those children born in the village that year; Samuel John Brough, Grace Frances Riley, Charlotte Emma Drake, Megan Little and Andrew Philip Tomkinson.

On Sunday, 7th July 2002, Monyash entered the electronic age when its web site was launched (www.monyash.info). This was designed for both villagers and visitors, providing plenty of information about the village and its facilities.

Box 29: Monyash in the National News

Monyash has hit the national news on several occasions. A road racing circuit that would have gone through Monyash was proposed in June 1955 and backed by Derbyshire County Council. However there was a good degree of opposition from, amongst others, the Council for the Protection of Rural England. The idea did not go ahead.[244] In April 1959 a jet aircraft crashed between Monyash and Flagg. Windows in the village shook with the impact and telegraph wires were brought down. The pilot and co-pilot managed to bail out and were taken to hospital suffering from shock and minor injuries.[245] In 1980 Miss Wood, who lived alone at Green Meadows on Cross Lane, disappeared while walking her dog. She was found about a year later in a gulley on the moors near Kinder Scout. In 1995 a hoard of more than 2,000 antiques, worth an estimated £350,000, were found at the 300-acre farm belonging to Alice Robinson after her death in February that year. Valuers found Georgian furniture, six long case clocks, chairs, lamps and pictures in the house and the outbuildings and reported that there was hardly room to move in the house because of all the antiques.[246] In 2009 a live hand grenade (a Mills bomb 36M) was dug up in the garden at The Croft, close to the village hall. Officers from the bomb squad blew the grenade up and warned that there may well be others. This was the site of a munitions dump during the Second World War.

Figure 78 St Leonard's Church before the second restoration

34. THE SECOND CHURCH RESTORATION

Figure 79
St Leonard's
Church after the
second restoration

In 1994 the Church was again in need of urgent repairs and the inside was dark and drab (see Figure 78). The Church has had little done to it since the major restoration by William Butterfield apart from general maintenance, including some re-pointing, repairs to roofs, the upgrading and maintenance of the heating system, maintenance of rainwater pipes and gutters and the relocation of the organ. The Parochial Church Council minutes reveal that a new organ was installed in the Church in 1925 (and rebuilt in 1953). One local farm boy (born and buried in Over Haddon) who frequently played the organ at Monyash became Sir Maurice Oldfield, chief of MI6, the Secret Intelligence Services, from 1973 to 1978.

Other work carried out since the Butterfield Restoration included some renovation and the screening off of the south transept to form a War Memorial Chapel sometime after the end of the First World War, though when this work was done is not clear. The architect is believed to have been P H Currey from Derby.[247] A plaque was erected in the Chapel in memory of the 12 villagers who lost their lives and in thanksgiving of the 33 who returned (the names and numbers are slightly different to those on the war memorial).

The spire was in need of renovation in 1923, some work finally being done in 1934. A lightening strike on the 14th July 1975 split off a piece of the spire, which is displayed in the Church. Some of the pews in the south aisle were also removed in the early 1980s.

On 3rd November 1995, maybe on the tide of the success of the IRD scheme, at a well attended village meeting in the village hall, a major project was launched to restore and renovate St Leonard's Church at an estimated cost of £120,000. It was hoped to complete the work in four years. About half of the work would be grant-aided by English Heritage and the Peak Park. The villagers had to raise the remainder. Graham Holland and Associates were engaged as the project's architects (see Figure 79 and Box 30: The 1996-2006 Restoration).

Box 30: The 1996-2006 Restoration

The Church of England's 1994 Quinquennial Review on St Leonard's Church revealed that there had been noticeable deterioration to the older parts of the building. Some of the stonework and pointing was crumbling, the tower had cracks in the walls, the lead work on the roof was corroded and the wiring was dilapidated. The Review made it clear that unless extensive renovations were undertaken in the near future the Church building would quickly deteriorate.

The work was to be completed in three stages. The first, largest and most urgent stage involved the repair of stonework in the tower, the insertion of ties to hold the two skins together and the re-pointing of the tower to prevent any further erosion. Phase one also involved the repair of the dilapidated timber screen in the south porch.

Phase one was begun at the end of July 1996 and finished on schedule on 15th November at a cost of around £62,000. This work allowed the bells to be heard once again, as previously they had been silent for fear of making the crack in the tower worse. The Bishop of Derby, the Right Rev Jonathan Bailey, led a service of celebration at the Church on 8th December.

The second phase involved the replacement or repair of all the crumbling stonework, mainly around the windows and doors in the chancel, south transept and the north aisle and the repointing of all the external stonework. At the same time the three bells, two of them dating from the early 20th century and the third from the 18th century, were restored to proper ringing condition and extensive repairs carried out to the ringing mechanism. New bell ropes were provided and the stair treads up to the bell and clock chambers made safe. The total cost was around £30,000.

The third phase involved the internal decoration and rewiring of the Church at cost of around £38,700. The whole of the electrical wiring and light fittings were renewed and, following a complete internal washing down of the walls and roof timbers, all of the rendered and plastered wall and ceiling surfaces lime washed. This phase was funded in part by a generous grant from the Derbyshire Churches and Chapels Preservation Trust. The final step was the replacement of the soft furnishings with new carpet runs complemented by a host of new individually embroidered kneelers. The opportunity was also taken to remove the pipe organ, a compact chamber instrument on wheels, from its position near to the north entrance to its former location between the vestry and pulpit, thus affording an uninterrupted view of the interior of the building upon entry to it from the north door. All of the pews and wood panelling were oiled and polished. The result has been to transform the interior appearance of the Church. While the project could not have been completed without the generosity of resident Sir William Blackburne, its achievement has been very much a village effort.

On 7th October 2007 a service of rededication to celebrate the refurbishment of the interior of the Church was led by the Bishop of Repton, the Rt Rev Humphrey Southern.

More recent renovations include a new heating boiler which was installed in 2009, at a cost of £11,700, and the renovation of the Royal Coat of Arms in 2010, at a cost of £2,400. There are plans to introduce a speech reinforcement system, to add piped water and drainage to allow for a toilet and kitchen area as well as the possibility of glazing the Lady Chapel to provide a warm venue for services in the winter.

35. MONYASH IN THE 21ST CENTURY

Monyash today is a reflection of its past, its history, but also its geology and geography. In many ways Monyash today is little different from how it was two thousand years ago. Then as now it was a small settlement, surrounded by fields bordered by stone walls and criss-crossed by paths, with its inhabitants working hard to keep their families. In other ways it is a very different place. Today there is relative peace where people, their families and their property, are no longer at risk from brutal invaders, or from cold and starvation. Survival is no longer the main concern. Prosperity and the welfare state provide some degree of relative comfort.

People have moved from a belief in a multitude of gods associated with fertility and food production, to a belief in several forms of Christianity, to an acceptance of several faiths, to a more secular society. Compared to 500 years ago, the Church and Chapel play only a small part in people's lives, in the main for funerals, christenings and weddings and other special occasions, such as Easter, Christmas, flower festivals and concerts.

Although remains of older buildings have long since disappeared, the look of the village has changed little in the last 100 years. Most of the dwellings are built in the traditional local style with limestone walls, gritstone details and stone slate roofs, and although very few have date stones, the majority are of 18th or early 19th century construction with some recent additions, such as Soldier's Croft and The Orchard. The oldest inhabited buildings may well be (parts of) The Bull i' th' Thorn (1471), The Bull's Head (1619), Ivy House (possibly 17th century), Post Office Farm (early 17th century), and Manor Farm (1714).

The village has many facilities, some would like more, but in these days of a market economy such things have to be justified and paid for. With a thriving school, a village hall, play park, pubs, the Smithy Café, the Church and Chapel, and an occasional bus service, Monyash appears to be very well served.

While farming is a key activity and reflects the nature of the village there are only a few farms and farmers looking after the many fields. Most of the village trades reported earlier have disappeared and some villagers travel many miles to work. Tourism, agriculture and quarrying are important local industries. Today mineral extraction is still an important industry in the area though lead mining has given way to limestone quarrying. The quarrying takes place in large open cast quarries some miles from the village, providing high quality limestone aggregates for commercial purposes. Fluorspar (calcium fluoride) used in steel, chemicals and ceramics industries, as well as road building, is mined extensively around the Peak District. Indeed Derbyshire fluorspar provides a significant amount of the national output.[248] This is transported by rail via Buxton (on the old LNWR railway line, see Box 27: The London and North Western Railway Company) and by road.

Tourism and farming (milk, beef and lamb) are the predominant industries of the area. Over the last 100 years there has been an upsurge in tourism in the area. The railways, and later the roads, opened up the Peak District as a place for recreation and leisure. It is well placed for many of the large cities, with Birmingham, Derby, Liverpool, Manchester, Nottingham and Sheffield all within easy reach. Indeed the Peak District is within an hour's journey for 16 million people – a third of the UK's population – and now has over 10 million visitors a year.[249]

The village amenities are now aimed at the tourists, in particular the many walkers and cyclists who come to explore and enjoy the hills and dales (see Box 28: Cycle Trails and Box 31: Flora and Fauna). They are well catered for by The Bull's Head and the Smithy Café, where the old smithy used to trade (see Figure 80). Several homes offer bed and breakfast accommodation and several houses are let as holiday cottages (for more information visit www.monyash.info). Although the village post office closed in 1996, the Church, the Chapel, The Bull's Head and the thriving primary school (with about 60 pupils) provide differing focal points for the inhabitants. Jack Mere is a car park and Cow Mere a playing field for the School, but Fere Mere remains and reminds us, as do the annual wells dressing, of the importance of water to life; and the reason for the existence of the village.

Figure 80 Monyash village green 2010

Box 31: Flora and Fauna

Almost every square mile of England has been affected by people – few wild and 'original' areas remain. Where there were once ancient forests there are now meadows and where there were commons there are fields, miles of dry stone walls and hillocks showing the location of previous mine workings. Each area has become a home for a variety of species of plants, birds and insects.

The area around Monyash contains a wide variety of wildflowers, insects, birds and small mammals. There are more than 40 species of wildflower around Monyash and in Lathkill Dale, which is a designated Site of Special Scientific Interest (SSSI) and a National Nature Reserve (NNR). The thin, well-drained soil is an ideal environment for many small plants and grasses such as the early purple orchid, wild garlic, liverwort, meadow cranesbill, cow parsley, cowslip, saxifrage and, one of Britain's rarest plants, Jacob's ladder. Many plants, known as metallophytes, such as alpine penny-cress, spring sandwort and maiden pink, are tolerant of heavy metals in the soil and so thrive around the old lead mine workings.

Insects such as grasshoppers, beetles, moths, glow-worms and butterflies thrive on the grasslands that are found in Lathkill Dale. Small mammals known to inhabit the area include bats, shrews, badgers, brown hares, stoats and weasels. A wide variety of birds can be found including sparrowhawks, owls, lapwings, curlews, house martins, swallows and many species of garden birds around the village as well as dippers in Lathkill Dale. There are also frogs, toads, slowworms and Great Crested Newts.

In recent years efforts have been made to re-introduce hay meadows in the area. It has been reckoned that 50 per cent of hay meadows were lost in the Peak District between the mid-1980s and the mid-1990s.[250] Established hay meadows support a diverse range of plants including ox-eye daisy, hay rattle, meadow vetchling and common knapweed. A programme of conservation of hay meadows began in 1995 by Natural England in partnership with Derbyshire Wildlife Trust and the National Park Authority. Two such sites have been preserved in Monyash, one at the head of the Dale (south side) and one along Hutmoor Butts.

REFERENCES

1 The information in this box is taken from English Nature (1996), *Lathkill Dale National Nature Reserve: Geology, English Nature*, Bakewell

2 http://www.thepeakdistrict.info/fast/html/volcanoes_of_the_peak_district.html

3 http://www.thepeakdistrict.info/fast/html/peak_district_mineralisation.html

4 http://www.thepeakdistrict.info/fast/html/volcanoes_of_the_peak_district.html

5 http://www.answersingenesis.org/home/area/fit/chapter9.asp

6 Bunting, Julie, (1992), Peak Advertiser, 30th March, vol. 13 no. 12

7 Cameron, K., (1959), "A Note on the Celtic Element in English Place-names", *Journal of the Derbyshire Archaeological and Natural History Society*, vol. 79, no. LXXIX, pp 56-60

8 Cox J. Charles, (1907), "The Church and Village of Monyash", *Journal of the Derbyshire Archaeological and Natural History Society*, vol.29, January, pp 1-20

9 This set of names is taken from Cameron, Kenneth, (1959), *The Place-names of Derbyshire, Part 1*, Cambridge University Press, Cambridge and James Pilkington, (1879), A View on the Present State of Derbyshire, vol. II, and Robert Morden's maps of Derbyshire, 1701 and 1722, http://eagle.cch.kcl.ac.uk:8080/cce/persons/CreatePersonFrames.jsp?PersonID=25919, http://eagle.cch.kcl.ac.uk:8080/cce/persons/CreatePersonFrames.jsp?PersonID=30517

10 Bryson, Bill, (1990), *Mother Tongue*, Penguin Books, p50

11 Bryson, Bill, (1990), *Mother Tongue*, Penguin Books

12 de la Mor la Souriete, Dame Cateline, A Survey of the History of English Place Names, http://www.sca.org/heraldry/laurel/names/engplnam.html

13 Mills, A. D., (1998), *A Dictionary of English Place-names*. 2nd ed., Oxford University Press, p 217

14 Jackson, Kenneth H., (1959), *Language and History in Early Britain*, as quoted in R.W.P. Cockerton "Celtic Influence in Derbyshire Place-names", *Journal of the Derbyshire Archaeological and Natural History Society*, vol. 79, no. LXXIX, pp 50-55

15 http://home.comcast.net/~modean52/oeme_dictionaries.htm

16 Cockerton, R.W.P., (1959), "Celtic Influence in Derbyshire Place-names", *Journal of the Derbyshire Archaelogical and Natural History Society*, vol. 79, no. LXXIX, pp 50-55

17 http://www.alphadictionary.com/directory/Languages/Celtic/

18 Cockerton, R.W.P., (1959), "Celtic Influence in Derbyshire Place-names", *Journal of the Derbyshire Archaeological and Natural History Society*, vol. 79, no. LXXIX, pp 50-55

19 http://www.utexas.edu/cola/centers/lrc/ielex/PokornyMaster-X.html

20 In the Palaeolithic Age (prior to 8500 BC) and the Mesolithic Age (c8500 – c3750 BC); see also Turbutt, Gladwyn, (1999), *A History of Derbyshire, vol. 1*, Merton Priory Press

21 English Nature, (1996), *Lathkill Dale National Nature Reserve*: History, English Nature, Bakewell and Castleden, Rodney, (1992), *Neolithic Britain: New Stone Age Sites of England, Scotland, and Wales*, Routledge

22 Turbutt, Gladwyn, (1999), *A History of Derbyshire, vol. 1*, Merton Priory Press

23 Turbutt, Gladwyn, (1999), *A History of Derbyshire, vol. 1*, Merton Priory Press, see also Chamberlain, A.T. and J.P. Williams, (2001), A Gazetteer of English Caves, Fissures and Rock Shelters Containing Human Remains. Revised version, available at http://capra.group.shef.ac.uk/1/caves.html

24 Barnatt, John and Ken Smith, (2004), *The Peak District: Landscapes Through Time*, Windgather Press, Macclesfield, Cheshire, p 5

25 http://www.idigsheffield.org.uk/index.asp?menu=expl

26 Turbutt, Gladwyn, (1999), *A History of Derbyshire, vol. 1*, Merton Priory Press

27 Turbutt, Gladwyn, (1999), *A History of Derbyshire, vol. 1*, Merton Priory Press

28 Bradley, Richard, (2007), *The Prehistory of Britain and Ireland*, Cambridge University Press

29 Parker, Frank, (2008), *Ancient Pathways*, unpublished booklet, Quarnford

30 Bradley, Richard, (2007), *The Prehistory of Britain and Ireland*, Cambridge University Press, p 17

31 Dodd, A.E. and E.M. Dodd, (2000), *Peakland Roads and Trackways*, Moorland Publishing

32 Mills, A. D., (1998), *A Dictionary of English Place-names*. 2nd ed., Oxford University Press and http://www.englandsnortheast.co.uk/PlaceNameMeaningsTtoY.html

33 Darvill, Timothy C., (1987), *Prehistoric Britain*, Routledge

34 Darvill, Timothy C., (1987), *Prehistoric Britain*, Routledge

35 Waterman, Christine (ed) (undated), *The Dover Bronze Age Boat*, The Bronze Age Boat Trust

36 Turbutt, Gladwyn, (1999), *A History of Derbyshire*, vol 1, Merton Priory Press

37 Turbutt, Gladwyn, (1999), *A History of Derbyshire, vol. 1*, Merton Priory Press

38 Turbutt, Gladwyn, (1999), *A History of Derbyshire, vol. 1*, Merton Priory Press, p 116

39 Barker, G.W.W., (1976), Stonehenge of the North: Arbor Low, Leaflet published by the Peak Park Joint Planning Board

40 Barnatt, John and Ken Smith, (2004), *The Peak District: Landscapes Through Time*, Windgather Press, Macclesfield, Cheshire

41 Barker, G.W.W., (1976), Stonehenge of the North: Arbor Low, Leaflet published by the Peak Park Joint Planning Board

42 Barnatt, John and Ken Smith, (2004), *The Peak District: Landscapes Through Time*, Windgather Press, Macclesfield, Cheshire

43 http://www.megalithic.co.uk/article.php?sid=0003

44   For more information visit http://www.bbc.co.uk/history/british/middle_ages/
45   For more information visit http://www.bbc.co.uk/history/british/middle_ages/
46   Marsden, Barry, (2007), "Iron Age Derbyshire", *Reflections*, vol. 16, no. 180, pp 26-28
47   http://www.peakdistrict-nationalpark.info/time/settlements/hillforts.html and Turbutt, Gladwyn, (1999), *A History of Derbyshire*, vol. 1, Merton Priory Press
48   Renfrew, Colin, (1990), *Archaeology and Language: The Puzzle of Indo-European Origins*. Cambridge: Cambridge University Press
49   Burgess, Colin, (2001), *The Age of Stonehenge*, Weidenfeld & Nicolson
50   Parker, Frank, (2008), Ancient Pathways, unpublished booklet, Quarnford
51   Green, Miranda J., (2005) *Exploring the world of the druids*. London: Thames & Hudson
52   Cunliffe, Barry, (2004), *Iron Age Britain*, Batsford Ltd
53   Green, Miranda J., (2005) *Exploring the world of the druids*. London: Thames & Hudson
54   Salway, Peter, (2000), *Roman Britain: A Very Short Introduction*, Oxford Paperbacks
55   Cunliffe, Barry, (2004), *Iron Age Britain*, Batsford Ltd
56   Turbutt, Gladwyn, (1999), *A History of Derbyshire*, vol. 1, Merton Priory Press, p 316
57   Christian, Roy, (1983), *Well-Dressing in Derbyshire*, Derbyshire Countryside Ltd
58   Christian, Roy, (1983), *Well-Dressing in Derbyshire*, Derbyshire Countryside Ltd
59   http://en.wikipedia.org/wiki/Derby
60   Dodd A.E. and E.M., Dodd (2000), *Peakland Roads and Trackways*, Moorland Publishing
61   The location given is Dry Dale though there is some uncertainty about which dale this might be. One suggestion is that this is the small dale running west of the village just south of, and parallel to, Tagg Lane. Turbutt, Gladwyn, (1999), *A History of Derbyshire*, vol. 1, Merton Priory Press
62   Barnatt, John and Ken Smith, (2004), *The Peak District: Landscapes Through Time*, Windgather Press, Macclesfield, Cheshire
63   English Nature, (1996), *Lathkill Dale National Nature Reserve: History*, English Nature, Bakewell, 1996
64   http://www.burkes-peerage.net/articles/roking01.aspx
65   http://en.wikipedia.org/wiki/List_of_monarchs_of_Mercia
66   http://www.hengistbury-head.co.uk/
67   Salway, Peter, (1981), *Roman Britain*, Oxford University Press, Oxford
68   http://www.bbc.co.uk/history/ancient/romans/overview_roman_01.shtml
69   Berresford Ellis, Peter, (1998), *The Ancient World of the Celts*, Constable and Company, London
70   McWhirr, Alan, (1982), *Roman Crafts and Industries*, Shire Publications, p 12
71   McWhirr, Alan, (1982), *Roman Crafts and Industries*, Shire Publications
72   Turbutt, Gladwyn, (1999), *A History of Derbyshire*, vol. 1, Merton Priory Press
73   Turbutt, Gladwyn, (1999), *A History of Derbyshire*, vol. 1, Merton Priory Press
74   Turbutt, Gladwyn, (1999), *A History of Derbyshire*, vol. 1, Merton Priory Press
75   Dodd, A.E. and E.M., Dodd (2000), *Peakland Roads and Trackways*, Moorland Publishing
76   Dodd, A.E. and E.M., Dodd (2000), *Peakland Roads and Trackways*, Moorland Publishing
77   Dodd, A.E. and E.M., Dodd (2000), *Peakland Roads and Trackways*, Moorland Publishing
78   Schama, Simon, (2000), *A History of Britain*, BBC Worldwide Ltd
79   Berresford Ellis, Peter, (1998), *The Ancient World of the Celts*, Constable and Company, London
80   http://www.wilfrid.com/Wilfrid_pilgrimage/Whitby_synod.htm
81   http://en.wikipedia.org/wiki/Easter#Computations
82   Crystal, David, (2003). *The Cambridge Encyclopedia of the English Language*. Cambridge University Press
83   Yorke, Barbara, (1990), *Kings and Kingdoms of Early Anglo-Saxon England*, Routledge
84   *New Scientist*, 28 June 2008, pp 52-53 and Else Roesdahl, (1991), The Vikings, Allen Lane, The Penguin Press, London
85   http://en.wikipedia.org/wiki/Derby
86   Roesdahl, Else, (1991), *The Vikings*, Allen Lane The Penguin Press, London
87   http://www.britannia.com/history/monarchs/saxons_wessex.html
88   Roesdahl, Else, (1991), *The Vikings*, Allen Lane The Penguin Press, London
89   For more information see Else Roesdahl, (1991), *The Vikings*, Allen Lane The Penguin Press, London
90   Roesdahl, Else, (1991), The Vikings, Allen Lane The Penguin Press, London
91   Ætheling means a person of royal blood, eligible for kingship, http://en.wikipedia.org/wiki/Ætheling
92   Wood, Michael, (1982), *In Search of the Dark Ages*, BBC, London
93   http://www.bbc.co.uk/history/british/normans/after_01.shtml
94   http://www.bbc.co.uk/history/british/normans/after_01.shtml
95   http://www.bbc.co.uk/history/british/normans/after_01.shtml
96   This translation was provided by Joy Davenport
97   Turbutt, Gladwyn, (1999), *A History of Derbyshire*, vol. 1, Merton Priory Press
98   http://en.wikipedia.org/wiki/Derbyshire
99   http://www.pilsburycastle.org.uk/
100   Wood, Michael, (1982), *In Search of the Dark Ages*, BBC, London
101   Page, William, (ed) (1910), "House of Cluniac monks: The priory of Lenton", *A History of the County of Nottingham*, vol. 2, pp. 91-100 http://www.british-history.ac.uk/report.aspx?compid=40086&strquery=monyash
102   http://www.burkes-peerage.net/

103   Turbutt, Gladwyn, (1999), *A History of Derbyshire*, vol. 2, Merton Priory Press, p 726
104   Page, William, (ed), (1910), "House of Cluniac monks: The priory of Lenton", *A History of the County of Nottingham*, vol. 2, pp 91-100
105   Turbutt, Gladwyn, (1999), *A History of Derbyshire*, vol. 2, Merton Priory Press, and http://www.wishful-thinking.org.uk/genuki/DBY/Eyam/Stafford/EyamJohnVI.html
106   http://en.wikipedia.org/wiki/Earl_of_Shrewsbury
107   Turbutt, Gladwyn, (1999), *A History of Derbyshire*, vol. 3, Merton Priory Press
108   Bagshawe, S., (1846), *History of Derbyshire*, p 448
109   Cox, J. Charles, (1907), "The Church and Village of Monyash", *Journal of the Derbyshire Archaeological and Natural History Society*, vol. 29, January, p 5
110   Turbutt, Gladwyn, (1999), *A History of Derbyshire*, vol. 2, Merton Priory Press
111   Cox, J. Charles, (1907), "The Church and Village of Monyash", *Journal of the Derbyshire Archaeological and Natural History Society*, vol. 29, January, p 12
112   http://www.catholic.org/saints/
113   Clapham, A. W. (1934), *English Romanesque Architecture: Before the Conquest and After the Conquest*, vol. 2
114   Cox, J. Charles, (1907), "The Church and Village of Monyash", *Journal of the Derbyshire Archaeological and Natural History Society*, vol. 29, January
115   Cox, J., Charles, (1886), *Catalogue of the Muniments of the Lichfield Vicars*, p158
      http://www.archive.org/stream/collectionsforhi188626staf/collectionsforhi188626staf_djvu.txt
116   Cox, J. Charles, (1876), "The Chapelry of Monyash", *Notes on the Churches of Derbyshire*, vol. 2, pp 105-111
117   Cox, J. Charles, (1907), "The Church and Village of Monyash", *Journal of the Derbyshire Archaeological and Natural History Society*, vol.29, January, pp 1-20
118   Turbutt, Gladwyn, (1999), *A History of Derbyshire*, vol. 1, Merton Priory Press
119   Turbutt, Gladwyn, (1999), *A History of Derbyshire*, vol. 1, Merton Priory Press
120   Cox J. Charles, (1876), "The Chapelry of Monyash", *Notes on the Churches of Derbyshire*, vol. 2, pp 105-111
121   Cox, J. Charles, (1907), "The Church and Village of Monyash", *Journal of the Derbyshire Archaeological and Natural History Society*, vol. 29, January, p 15
122   Cox, J., Charles, (1886), *Catalogue of the Muniments of the Lichfield Vicars*
      http://www.archive.org/stream/collectionsforhi188626staf/collectionsforhi188626staf_djvu.txt
123   http://www.archive.org/stream/journalofderbysh28derb/journalofderbysh28derb_djvu.txt
124   Cox, J. Charles, (1907), "The Church and Village of Monyash", *Journal of the Derbyshire Archaeological and Natural History Society*, vol. 29, January, pp 1-20
125   Cox, J. Charles, (1907), "The Church and Village of Monyash", *Journal of the Derbyshire Archaeological and Natural History Society*, vol. 29, January, pp 19
126   Cox, J. Charles, (1907), "The Church and Village of Monyash", *Journal of the Derbyshire Archaeological and Natural History Society*, vol. 29, January, p 17
127   Cox, J. Charles, (1907), "The Church and Village of Monyash", *Journal of the Derbyshire Archaeological and Natural History Society*, vol. 29, January, pp 1-20
128   Elton, G. R., (1991), *England Under the Tudors*, Routledge
129   Turbutt, Gladwyn, (1999), *A History of Derbyshire*, vol. 2, Merton Priory Press
130   Cox, J. Charles, (1907), "The Church and Village of Monyash", *Journal of the Derbyshire Archaeological and Natural History Society*, vol. 29, January, pp 1-20
131   Turbutt, Gladwyn, *A History of Derbyshire*, vol 2, Merton Priory Press, 1999
132   Cox, J. Charles, (1907), "The Church and Village of Monyash", *Journal of the Derbyshire Archaeological and Natural History Society*, vol. 29, January, pp 1-20
133   Cox, J. Charles, (1907), "The Church and Village of Monyash", *Journal of the Derbyshire Archaeological and Natural History Society*, vol. 29, January, pp 1-20
134   Davies, D.P. (1811), *A New Historical and Descriptive View of Derbyshire*, p 608
135   Peak Advertiser, (1992), vol. 10 no. 5, 16 March
136   Cox, J. Charles, (1907), "The Church and Village of Monyash", *Journal of the Derbyshire Archaeological and Natural History Society*, vol.29, January, pp 1-20
137   White, Frances and Co., (1857), *History, Gazetteer and Directory of the County of Derby*, Frances White and Co., electronic copy available from http://www.n.f.wilson.btinternet.co.uk/
138   Lindsey Porter and http://en.wikipedia.org/wiki/Barmote_court
139   Turbutt, Gladwyn, (1999), *A History of Derbyshire*, vol. 2, Merton Priory Press
140   http://en.wikipedia.org/wiki/Derbyshire_lead_mining_history
141   Turbutt, Gladwyn, (1999), *A History of Derbyshire*, vol. 1, Merton Priory Press
142   Rieuwerts, James H.,(1973) *Lathkill Dale: its mines and miners*, Moorland Publishing, Ashbourne, Derbyshire
143   Rieuwerts, James H.,(1973) *Lathkill Dale: its mines and miners*, Moorland Publishing, Ashbourne, Derbyshire
144   Rieuwerts, James H.,(1973) *Lathkill Dale: its mines and miners*, Moorland Publishing, Ashbourne, Derbyshire
145   Rieuwerts, James H.,(1973) *Lathkill Dale: its mines and miners*, Moorland Publishing, Ashbourne, Derbyshire
146   White, Frances and Co., (1857), *History, Gazetteer and Directory of the County of Derby*, Frances White and Co., electronic copy available from http://www.n.f.wilson.btinternet.co.uk/
147   English Nature, (1996), *Lathkill Dale National Nature Reserve*: History, English Nature, Bakewell
148   Worley, Noel E., T. Worthington and L Riley, (1978), "The Geology and Exploration of the Hubbadale Mines, Taddington",

Peak District Mines Historical Society, vol. 7, no. 1, pp 31-39

149   Holmes, Robin and Allan J Farley, (2006), *Dear Sister: Letters between a pioneer Wairarapa family and relatives in rural England*, Wairarapa Archive

150   Buckley R., and M. Howard, (1995), "Greensward Mine and its Pumps, Monyash, Derbyshire", *Bulletin of the Peak District Mines Historical Society*, vol. 12, no. 6, pp 68-81

151   Willies, Lynn, (1990), *Magpie Mine: A Guide for Visitors*, Peak District Mining Museum

152   Willies, Lynn, (1990), *Magpie Mine: A Guide for Visitors*, Peak District Mining Museum

153   Porter, Lindsey, (2007), *Lost Buildings of the Peak District*, The Horizon Press

154   Cox, J. Charles, (1907), "The Church and Village of Monyash", *Journal of the Derbyshire Archaeological and Natural History Society*, vol. 29, January, p3

155   Cox, J. Charles, (1907), "The Church and Village of Monyash", *Journal of the Derbyshire Archaeological and Natural History Society*, vol. 29, January

156   http://www.bulliththorn.co.uk

157   http://www.n.f.wilson.btinternet.co.uk/

158   Dodd, A.E. and E.M., Dodd, (2000), *Peakland Roads and Trackways*, Moorland Publishing

159   Radley, Jeffrey, "Peak District Roads Prior to The Turnpike Era", *Derbyshire Archaeological Journal*, vol. LXXXIII, July 1964, pp 39-50

160   http://www.milestonesweb.com/features/guidestoops.htm

161   Smith, Howard, (2009), *The Guide Stoops of Derbyshire*, Landmark Collector's Library, Horizon Press, Ashbourne

162   Dodd, A.E. and E.M., Dodd, (2000), *Peakland Roads and Trackways*, Moorland Publishing, also from J. Charles Cox (1907), "The Church and Village of Monyash", *Journal of the Derbyshire Archaeological and Natural History Society*, vol. 29, January, pp 1-20 and Julie Bunting (2009), "Without the sight of any earth", Peak Advertiser, 23 February, p 15

163   Dodd, A.E. and E.M., Dodd, (2000), *Peakland Roads and Trackways*, Moorland Publishing

164   Jeavons, S.A., 1964, "Royal Arms in Derbyshire Churches", *Derbyshire Archaeological Journal*, vol. LXXXIII, pp 51-65

165   Askey, Mark, (1996), The Restoration of the Church of St Leonard, Monyash, unpublished paper

166   http://www.n.f.wilson.btinternet.co.uk/

167   http://www.n.f.wilson.btinternet.co.uk/

168   White, Frances and Co., (1857), *History, Gazetteer and Directory of the County of Derby*, Frances White and Co., electronic copy available from http://www.n.f.wilson.btinternet.co.uk/

169   Elliott, N., (1986), *Village Odyssey: Exploring Villages from Manchester*, Churchman Publishing

170   Turbutt, Gladwyn, (1991), *A History of Derbyshire*, vol. 3, Merton Priory Press

171   http://www.quaker.org.uk

172   Bunting, Julie, (1997), "Quakers in the Peak District", *Peak Advertiser*, vol. 15, no. 10, May

173   Turbutt, Gladwyn, (1999), *A History of Derbyshire*, vol. 3, Merton Priory Press

174   Turbutt, Gladwyn, (1999), *A History of Derbyshire*, vol. 3, Merton Priory Press

175   Turbutt, Gladwyn, (1999), *A History of Derbyshire*, vol. 3, Merton Priory Press and based on a story told by Rev. Jim Hildage

176   Gratton, John, (1795), *A Journal in the Life of That Ancient Servant of Christ, John Gratton*, pp xii-xiii

177   Bagshawe, S., (1846), *History of Derbyshire*, p 449

178   http://www.hallvworthington.com/Gratton/Gratton-5.html

179   Turbutt, Gladwyn, (1999), *A History of Derbyshire*, vol. 4, Merton Priory Press, p 1574

180   http://www.archive.org/stream/themakersofwesl00pilkuoft/themakersofwesl00pilkuoft_djvu.txt

181   http://www.stevelewis.me.uk/page18.php

182   *Derbyshire Times*, (1973), January 26th

183   Turbutt, Gladwyn, (1999), *A History of Derbyshire*, vol. 4, Merton Priory Press

184   http://www.spartacus.schoolnet.co.uk/REmethodism.htm

185   http://www.britishplate.org.uk/johncheney/johncheney.html

186   Smith, Roy, (2010), "Of Norman Descent", *Reflections Magazine*, vol. 17 no. 219, pp 52-55

187   http://www.britishplate.org.uk/johncheney/johncheney.html

188   Holmes, Robin and Allan J Farley, (2006), *Dear Sister: Letters between a pioneer Wairarapa family and relatives in rural England*, Wairarapa Archive

189   Holmes, Robin and Allan J Farley, (2006), *Dear Sister: Letters between a pioneer Wairarapa family and relatives in rural England*, Wairarapa Archive

190   Bagshawe, S., (1846), *History of Derbyshire*, p 448

191   The Reliquary, (1870), Extracts from the Parish Registers of Monyash and Taddington, Derbyshire, vol. 11

192   White, Frances and Co., (1857), *History, Gazetteer and Directory of the County of Derby*, Frances White and Co., electronic copy available from http://www.n.f.wilson.btinternet.co.uk/

193   Bagshawe, S., (1846), *History of Derbyshire*, p 449

194   From a translated copy of the original 1752 agreement

195   Derbyshire transcripts of Kelly's (1891) Directory from Kelly's Directory of the Counties of Derby, Notts, Leicester and Rutland, London, May, p.267

196   Derbyshire transcripts of Kelly's (1891) Directory from Kelly's Directory of the Counties of Derby, Notts, Leicester and Rutland, London, May, p.267

197   Cox, J. Charles, (1907), "The Church and Village of Monyash", *Journal of the Derbyshire Archaeological and Natural History Society*, vol. 29, January, pp 21

198   Turbutt, Gladwyn, (1999), *A History of Derbyshire*, vol. 2, Merton Priory Press

199   http://www.peakdistrict-nationalpark.info/time/limestone/stripFields.html
200   The Monyash Enclosure Act, 1771
201   Barnatt, John and Ken Smith, (2004), *The Peak District: Landscapes Through Time*, Windgather Press, Macclesfield, Cheshire
202   The Monyash Enclosure Act, 1771
203   Holmes, Robin and Allan J Farley, (2006), *Dear Sister: Letters between a pioneer Wairarapa family and relatives in rural England*, Wairarapa Archive
204   Derbyshire transcripts of Kelly's (1891) Directory from Kelly's Directory of the Counties of Derby, Notts, Leicester and Rutland. London, May, p.267
205   Derbyshire Hearth Tax Assessments 1662-70, (1982), *Derbyshire Record Society*, vol. VII
206   Derbyshire Hearth Tax Assessments 1662-70, (1982), *Derbyshire Record Society*, vol. VII
207   Pilkington, James, (1879), *A View on the Present State of Derbyshire*, vol. II
208   Bagshawe, S., (1846), *History of Derbyshire*
209   Bagshawe, S., (1857), *History of Derbyshire*, 2nd edition
210   Parker, Ken, (1984) The Story of the Integrated Rural Development Experiment in the Peak District, 1981-1984, Peak Park Joint Planning Board
211   Parker, Ken, (1990), Two Villages Two Valleys, Peak Park Joint Planning Board, Bakewell
212   Bagshawe, S., (1846), *History of Derbyshire*, p 450
213   Kelly's (1891), Directory of the Counties of Derby, Notts, Leicester and Rutland, London May, p 267
214   Holmes, Robin and Allan J Farley, (2006), *Dear Sister: Letters between a pioneer Wairarapa family and relatives in rural England*, Wairarapa Archive
215   http://www.nationalarchives.gov.uk/records/census-records.htm
216   Barnatt, John and Ken Smith, (2004), *The Peak District: Landscapes Through Time*, Windgather Press, Macclesfield, Cheshire
217   English Nature, (1996), *Lathkill Dale National Nature Reserve:* History, English Nature, Bakewell
218   Cox, J. Charles, (1907), "The Church and Village of Monyash", *Journal of the Derbyshire Archaeological and Natural History Society*, vol. 29, January, pp 1-20
219   Barton, D., and L. Knighton, (1997), *Britain in Old Photographs: Around Bakewell*, Sutton Publishing Ltd
220   Askey, Mark, (1996), The Restoration of the Church of St Leonard, Monyash, unpublished paper
221   Askey, Mark, (1996), The Restoration of the Church of St Leonard, Monyash, unpublished paper
222   Askey, Mark, (1996), The Restoration of the Church of St Leonard, Monyash, unpublished paper
223   Askey, Mark, (1996), The Restoration of the Church of St Leonard, Monyash, unpublished paper
224   Cox, J. Charles, (1907), "The Church and Village of Monyash", *Journal of the Derbyshire Archaeological and Natural History Society*, vol. 29, January,pp 1-20
225   Jones, Norman, and J. Michael Bentley, (2001), *Railways of the High Peak: Onwards to Cromford and High Peak Junction*, Foxline, Stockport
226   Jones, Norman, and J. Michael Bentley, (2000), *Railways of the High Peak: Whaley Bridge to Friden*, Foxline, Stockport
227   Jones, Norman., and J. Michael Bentley (2000), *Railways of the High Peak: Whaley Bridge to Friden*, Foxline, Stockport
228   http://railways-of-britain.com/CHPR.html
229   Jones, Norman, and J. Michael Bentley (2000), *Railways of the High Peak: Whaley Bridge to Friden*, Foxline, Stockport
230   Peak Advertiser, (1992), vol. 10 no. 5, 16 March
231   Peak Advertiser, (1992), vol. 10 no. 5, 16 March
232   Daily Mail, (1975), November 17th, p9
233   www.1911census.co.uk
234   Parker H.M. and L. Willies, (1979), *Peakland Lead Mines and Miners*, Moorland Publishing
235   Bentley, J. Michael. and Gregory K. Fox, (1997), *Railways of the High Peak: Buxton to Ashbourne*, Foxline Publications, Stockport
236   Bentley, J. Michael. and Gregory K. Fox, (1997), *Railways of the High Peak: Buxton to Ashbourne*, Foxline Publications, Stockport
237   http://www.subbrit.org.uk/sb-sites/stations/p/parsley_hay/index.shtml
238   Parker, Ken, (1984), A Tale of Two Villages, Peak Park Joint Planning Board, Bakewell and Parker, Ken, (1990), Two Villages Two Valleys, Peak Park Joint Planning Board, Bakewell
239   Parker, Ken, (1990), Two Villages Two Valleys, Peak Park Joint Planning Board, Bakewell
240   http://www.europanostra.org/lang_en/index.html
241   Parker, Ken, (1984), A Tale of Two Villages, Peak Park Joint Planning Board, Bakewell
242   Parker, Ken, (1984), A Tale of Two Villages, Peak Park Joint Planning Board, Bakewell
243   http://www.whitepeakwalk.co.uk
244   The Times, 16th June 1955
245   *Buxton Advertiser*, (2009), March 3rd, from the column 50 years ago, and The Times, 10th April, 1958
246   *The Times*, 21st August 1995, p 5
247   Askey, Mark, (1996), The Restoration of the Church of St Leonard, Monyash, unpublished paper
248   Turbutt, Gladwyn, (1999), *A History of Derbyshire*, vol. 1, Merton Priory Press
249   www.peakdistrict.gov.uk
250   http://www.peakdistrict.gov.uk/index/looking-after/bap/bap-publications/bap-action-hm.htm

INDEX